re

Pasta

Pasta

Over 70 quick
and easy recipes

hamlyn

A Pyramid Paperback

First published in Great Britain in 2006 by Hamlyn,
a division of Octopus Publishing Group Ltd,
2–4 Heron Quays, London E14 4JP

ISBN-13: 978-0-600-61453-1
ISBN-10: 0-600-61453-0

A CIP catalogue record for this book is available
from the British Library

Printed and bound in China

10 9 8 7 6 5 4 3 2 1

Notes

Both metric and imperial measurements have
been given in all recipes. Use one set of
measurements only and not a mixture of both.

Meat and poultry should be cooked thoroughly.
To test if poultry is cooked, pierce the flesh
through the thickest part with a skewer or fork –
the juices should run clear, never pink or red.

This book includes dishes made with nuts and
nut derivatives. It is advisable for those with
known allergic reactions to nuts and nut
derivatives and those who may be potentially
vulnerable to these allergies, such as pregnant
and nursing mothers, invalids, the elderly, babies
and children, to avoid dishes made with nuts and
nut oils. It is also prudent to check the labels of
pre-prepared ingredients for the possible
inclusion of nut derivatives.

The Department of Health advises that eggs
should not be consumed raw. This book contains
some dishes made with raw or lightly cooked eggs.
It is prudent for more vulnerable people, such as
pregnant and nursing mothers, invalids, the elderly,
babies and young children, to avoid uncooked or
lightly cooked dishes made with eggs.

Contents

Types of pasta

Delicious, healthy, quick to cook and, above all, economical – pasta really is the ultimate convenience food. Whether simply tossed with a sauce, fresh vegetables or salad ingredients, or combined as a dish and baked in the oven, pasta can be used as the base of countless fabulous meals. And because there are so many different types of pasta – fresh or dried, long or short, stuffed or flat – and so many ways of combining them, from the ultra-simple to the impressively sophisticated, there really is a pasta dish for every occasion.

Of the many, many different types of pasta available, they can be divided into four main categories: long, short, flat and stuffed. In turn, these may be fresh or dried, with wholemeal varieties available in some shapes, and made of durum wheat flour and

water, or with additional egg (all'uovo). They may also be coloured and flavoured with spinach (green), tomato (red), beetroot (pink), saffron (yellow), squid ink (black) and herbs.

Fresh pasta is delicious, although not necessarily better than dried pasta – and many Italians will choose dried pasta over fresh for specific dishes. As a rule of thumb, buy the best pasta you can afford, as it will make all the difference to the final flavour and texture of the dish.

LONG PASTA

Most types of long pasta are sold dried, and some are also available fresh. They vary in length and may be sold in straight lengths, pressed into waves or coiled into nests. They are usually made from plain durum wheat. Those made with delicate egg pasta are usually sold coiled into nests. Most long pastas suit smooth, creamy and clinging sauces. Common varieties include:

• **Bucatini** Resembling a thick spaghetti, each strand is hollow. There is a thicker version known as bucatoni.

• **Capelli d'angelo** Also called angel hair pasta, this very long, thin pasta is like a delicate vermicelli and is sold in nests. It is usually served with sauce, or in soup.

• **Fettuccine** Long, flat ribbons sold in nests. It may be plain, with egg or with spinach. It can be used interchangeably with tagliatelle.

• **Linguine** Resembling a thin, flat spaghetti and used in the same way.

• **Pappardelle** Broad, flat noodles, often with a wavy edge. It is often made with egg pasta and is traditionally served with meat and game sauces.

- **Spaghetti** Probably the best known of all long pastas, these long, thin strings are good with any sauce. Spaghettini has thinner strands.
- **Tagliatelle** Flat ribbon noodles sold in nests. It may be plain or with egg or spinach.
- **Vermicelli** Fine pasta strands, sold coiled into nests. It may be plain or with egg and is good with light sauces.

SHORT PASTA

There are even more varieties of short pasta than there are long. They are widely available fresh and dried and may be plain, with egg, or flavoured and coloured. They are favoured by many for their versatility – suiting most sauces and being great in salads and baked dishes. Common varieties include:
- **Conchiglie** Shell-shaped and available in many different sizes – from large ones for stuffing, medium ones for tossing with sauce and tiny ones for soup.
- **Farfalle** Little pasta bows, plain or flavoured with spinach or tomato.
- **Fiorelli** Pretty pasta tubes with a lacy edge.
- **Fusilli** Spirals resembling tight springs, formed by wrapping dough around a thin rod.
- **Macaroni** Thick, slightly curved tubes of pasta. It is particularly popular served with thick, creamy sauces and in baked dishes.
- **Pastina** Tiny pasta shapes for soup. They come in a fabulous array of shapes including stars, letters, tubes, shells, bows, rings and squares. Larger ones are good for chunky soups such as minestrone, while the tiniest are ideal for light broths.
- **Penne** Tubular pasta shapes with angled ends, resembling a quill.

- **Rigatoni** Ridged, chunky tubes used in the same way as macaroni.
- **Rotelle** Shaped like tiny cartwheels, these are very popular with children.

FLAT PASTA

There are many flat pasta ribbons (see long pasta, above), but there is really only one type of flat pasta sheet.
- **Lasagne** Usually plain or flavoured with spinach, and available dried or fresh. The most commonly available varieties require no pre-cooking. The flat or ridged sheets may be layered with sauce and baked to make classic lasagne, or cooked then rolled around a filling and baked to make cannelloni.

STUFFED PASTA

Usually available fresh, but also dried, stuffed pasta is good served simply, tossed with butter or oil, or with smooth sauces. Common varieties include:
- **Cannelloni** Dried pasta tubes for stuffing yourself, then covering in sauce and baking.
- **Cappelletti** Little hat-shaped pasta shapes made from a square of pasta dough that has been filled, folded into a triangle, and the ends wrapped round to make a 'brim'. Traditionally eaten at Christmas in broth, but also good tossed with butter or sauce.
- **Ravioli** Usually square, these stuffed cushions of pasta may be large or small. Fillings may vary, too, with meat, fish, shellfish, cheese and vegetables all being popular.
- **Tortellini** Similar in appearance to cappelletti, although larger and made with dough rounds rather than squares. Like ravioli, fillings are many and varied.

Cooking pasta

Pasta, whether fresh or dried, is incredibly simple to cook – as long as you follow these simple rules.

1 Always use a big pan with plenty of water. The pasta needs enough room to cook without sticking together. Allow about 5 litres (8 pints) of water for every 500 g (1 lb) of pasta. If you're cooking less pasta, you should still use at least 2.75 litres (5 pints) of water.

2 Add enough salt to the water: pasta cooked in unsalted water will give tasteless results. Allow 1½–2 tablespoons of salt for every 500 g (1 lb) of pasta. (Don't worry if this sounds like a lot of salt; most of it will be thrown away with the cooking water.)

3 Add a little oil to the water to prevent the pasta sticking together. In the case of lasagne sheets, up to a tablespoonful of oil may be needed. (Note that this oil will not be listed in each recipe's ingredients.) Bring the cooking water to a fast rolling boil before adding the pasta – otherwise the pasta can become stodgy.

4 Add the pasta in one go so that it all has the same cooking time. Long pasta such as spaghetti should be placed in the boiling water, then gently pressed into the water as it softens to ensure even cooking.

5 Give the pasta a quick stir to prevent it sticking together, then quickly return the water to a rolling boil.

6 Reduce the heat to medium-high so that the water remains at a brisk boil, stirring now and again to prevent the pasta sticking.

7 The pasta is ready when it is al dente – that is tender, yet still with a bite when bitten. The easiest way to check this is to remove a piece of pasta from the pan and give it a bite. If you overcook pasta, you will get soft, stodgy results.

8 As soon as the pasta is al dente, drain it well, shaking the colander or sieve to remove any excess water. Reserve 2–3 tablespoons of cooking water in case you need to loosen the pasta sauce when you combine it with the pasta. (If the pasta is to be served cold, rinse it under cold water in the colander, then set aside.)

9 Serve immediately with the sauce of your choice, or add to ingredients ready for baking.

HOW MUCH PASTA?

The quantity of pasta required per person is a slightly moveable feast, depending on appetite, whether the sauce is light or substantial, and whether you're serving the dish as an appetizer or main course. However, you can use the following dry weight as a general guide:

- **for an appetizer**, allow 50 g (2 oz) per person
- **for a main meal**, allow 75–125 g (3–4 oz) per person.

COOKING TIMES

Accurate timing is essential for perfect pasta, and cooking times can vary according to the variety, brand and type of pasta. Always check the packet for timing, or, if you're making your own, follow the timing given in the recipe. Start timing as soon as the water returns to the boil after adding the pasta. As a general guide, use the following times:

- **thin, fresh noodles** 1–2 minutes
- **thicker fresh noodles and pasta shapes** 2–3 minutes
- **stuffed fresh pasta** 3–4 minutes
- **dried pasta** 8–12 minutes (though wholemeal may take longer).

WHICH PASTA? WHAT SAUCE?

Another secret to success when serving pasta is pairing the right pasta with the right sauce – and synchronizing your timing so that they're both ready at the same time. (Most sauces can stand a little waiting while the pasta finishes cooking, but pasta is best served as soon as it is cooked, so try to make sure your sauce is ready in time.)

Although some sauces are traditionally served with specific pastas – for example *fettuccine all'Alfredo*, *bucatini all'Amatriciana*, and *penne all'Arrabiata* – common sense usually prevails when pairing pasta and sauces.

Heavy, chunky sauces are best served with short pasta shapes, such as penne, conchiglie and rigatoni, or wide noodles, such as pappardelle and tagliatelle. The sauce doesn't slide off these pastas in the way that it would with long smooth spaghetti, or overpower it in the way that it would a fine, delicate pasta such as capelli d'angelo.

Long, thin pastas, such as spaghetti and linguine, go better with smooth sauces that cling to their length, such as tomato or creamy sauces. And delicate pastas such as vermicelli go well with light sauces, such as seafood ones.

There are also classic Italian regional pairings. For example, olive oil sauces made with tomatoes and seafood, which are popular in the south, are usually served with the plain durum wheat pasta, such as spaghetti and vermicelli, that is popular in the area. In the north, however, sauces are frequently made with butter and cream, and these go very well with the egg pasta that is made there.

STORAGE

Fresh pasta is best eaten on the day that it is made, although it can be refrigerated for 24 hours, or frozen for up to 3 months. Ready-made, vacuum-packed varieties may be stored in the refrigerator for slightly longer, so check the advice on the packet. Once opened, dried pasta should be stored in an airtight container and used within 9 months.

Basic pasta recipes

MAKING FRESH EGG PASTA

Fresh pasta is easy to make and tastes delicious. For the best results, look out for the special Italian flour Farina Bianco 00 or Tipo 00, available from Italian delicatessens. Failing that, use strong white bread flour. Plain flour will not give the same results.

Depending on the type of flour you use and the humidity, you may need slightly more or less flour. The dough should be fairly hard to knead, but be careful not to add too much flour as this will give tough, floury results. This recipe gives quantities for 2–4 people, depending on appetite, sauce and whether serving as a main course or appetizer.

200 g (7 oz) Farina Bianco 00 or Tipo 00
pinch of salt
2 large eggs, beaten
1 tablespoon olive oil

1 Sift the flour and salt in a mound on a clean work surface and make a well in the centre.
2 Beat together the eggs and olive oil and pour the mixture into the well. Using your fingers, gradually mix the eggs into the flour, then bring it together to form a dough.
3 Knead the pasta for about 10 minutes until smooth, then wrap in clingfilm and leave to rest for at least 30 minutes before rolling out.

MAKING FLAVOURED PASTA

There are several variations on the basic pasta dough above, all of which will produce delicious, colourful results.

- **Spinach pasta** Sift the flour on to the work surface as before. Cook 150 g (5 oz) frozen leaf spinach and squeeze out as much liquid as possible. Put it into a food processor or blender with the salt and eggs and process until smooth. Pour the mixture into the flour and proceed as before.
- **Tomato pasta** Add 2 tablespoons of tomato purée to the flour and use 2 small or medium eggs.
- **Beetroot pasta** Add 2 tablespoons of grated cooked beetroot to the flour and use 2 small or medium eggs.
- **Saffron pasta** Soak a sachet of powdered saffron in 2 tablespoons of hot water for 15 minutes. Whisk the saffron water with 2 small or medium eggs, then add to the flour.
- **Herb pasta** Add 3 tablespoons of chopped fresh herbs, such as basil, to the flour.
- **Black pasta** Add 1 sachet of squid ink (available from Italian delicatessens) to the eggs before adding them to the flour. You may need to add a little extra flour.

ROLLING PASTA

The simplest way to roll pasta is to use a pasta machine, although if you don't have one, you can roll it out using a rolling pin. If you have made more pasta than you can roll at one time, keep the remainder covered with a damp cloth to prevent it drying out.

1 Feed the rested pasta dough through the widest setting on the machine, folding it in three. Repeat another two times, then feed the

pasta through the machine, reducing the settings each time until you reach the required thickness. As a general rule, the second to last setting is best for tagliatelle, and the final setting for filled pasta such as ravioli.

2 To make tagliatelle, hang the rolled dough over a wooden pasta stand or broom handle to dry a little. Pass the slightly dried pasta through the chosen cutter and transfer to a baking tray covered with a clean tea towel sprinkled with a little flour. Toss the pasta to coat in the flour and cook as soon as possible. Alternatively, hang the pasta over the stand or broom handle again until ready to cook.

3 To make ravioli or other stuffed pasta, do not allow the rolled pasta to dry out but fill and shape immediately, as the dough needs to be slightly tacky to stick to itself.

SIMPLE PASTA SAUCES

As well as the more complex pasta sauces provided in the recipe section of this book, there are a variety of easy to prepare, no-fuss sauces that can transform simple boiled pasta into a delicious meal. Here are two tasty examples.

Spaghetti with garlic, chilli and oil

This classic Roman dish is served as it is, with no need for additional pepper or cheese. While the spaghetti cooks, heat 6 tablespoons of oil in a frying pan. Add 3 crushed garlic cloves and 1 dried chilli and stir over a low heat until the garlic is just starting to brown. Remove the chilli, then pour the garlicky oil over the drained spaghetti. Add a small handful of chopped parsley, toss together and serve.

Fettucine with butter and Parmesan

A classic northern dish, this simple way of serving pasta will be a hit with the whole family. Add 50 g (2 oz) unsalted butter to freshly cooked fettucine and toss well until melted. Sprinkle over 125 g (4 oz) grated Parmesan and toss again to combine. Season with black pepper and serve.

INSTANT SAUCES FOR SPEEDY MEALS

There are plenty of ready-made pasta sauces available that can be stored in the refrigerator, freezer or storecupboard. Try a few of the following, tossing in some steamed vegetables and perhaps some ham or fish, to make delicious instant meals.

- **Pesto** this simple Genoese sauce made with Parmesan, basil and pine nuts is delicious tossed with plain pasta. There is also a red version made with sun-dried tomatoes.
- **Cheese sauce** fresh or bottled, this is a great standby and can be dressed up with other ingredients such as steamed broccoli. Either toss with pasta and serve as it is, or transfer to a baking dish, sprinkle over a little cheese and bake until brown and bubbling.
- **Tomato sauce** fresh or bottled, this is another great standby that's good combined with extra ingredients. Canned fish, spicy chilli and roasted peppers are all excellent additions.

Sauces

Tuck into a hearty bolognese with spicy sausage, toss together a simple tomato and bacon sauce for a speedy supper, or indulge yourself with a lusciously creamy Gorgonzola sauce. Whatever food you're in the mood for, there's always a perfect sauce.

serves **4**
preparation time **5 minutes**
cooking time **15 minutes**

Tomato and bacon sauce

2 garlic cloves, crushed
2 x 400 g (13 oz) cans chopped
  tomatoes
4 tablespoons extra virgin
  olive oil
1 teaspoon dried oregano
1 teaspoon caster sugar
8 rashers of smoked back
  bacon, finely chopped
75 g (3 oz) mascarpone cheese
  or 75 ml (3 fl oz) crème
  fraîche
salt and pepper

1 Put the garlic, tomatoes, oil, oregano and sugar in a saucepan. Season to taste with salt and pepper and bring to the boil. Cover and simmer for 10 minutes.

2 Add the bacon and simmer, uncovered, for a further 5 minutes.

3 Stir in the mascarpone or crème fraîche, heat through then taste and adjust the seasoning if necessary. Serve with freshly cooked pasta.

PASTA TIP
This is a good basic sauce for pasta and can be made without the bacon for vegetarians. You can make up several batches, minus the mascarpone or crème fraîche, and freeze it for future use.

serves **2**
preparation time **8 minutes**
cooking time **15 minutes**

Anchovy and oregano sauce

1 tablespoon olive oil
2 garlic cloves, finely
    chopped
50 g (2 oz) anchovy fillets in
    oil, drained and chopped
2 teaspoons oregano, finely
    chopped
pepper
3 tablespoons chopped
    parsley, to garnish
freshly grated Parmesan
    cheese, to serve

1 Heat the oil in a small saucepan, add the garlic and fry gently for about 5 minutes until golden.

2 Reduce the heat to very low, stir in the anchovies and cook very gently for about 10 minutes until they have completely disintegrated.

3 Stir in the oregano and pepper to taste.

4 Serve with freshly cooked pasta, sprinkled with parsley and Parmesan.

serves **4**
preparation time **12 minutes**
cooking time **15 minutes**

Puttanesca sauce

4 tablespoons olive oil
1 onion, finely chopped
3 garlic cloves, crushed
1 small red chilli, deseeded
and finely chopped
6 anchovy fillets in oil, drained
and chopped
2 x 400 g (13 oz) cans chopped
tomatoes
½ teaspoon caster sugar
75 g (3 oz) pitted black olives,
finely chopped
small handful of basil leaves,
torn into small pieces
2 tablespoons capers, rinsed
and drained
salt
freshly grated Parmesan
cheese, to serve (optional)

1 Heat the oil in a heavy-based saucepan. Add the onion and fry gently for 3–4 minutes until softened. Add the garlic and chilli and cook for a further minute.

2 Add the anchovy fillets, tomatoes, sugar and black olives, and bring to the boil. Reduce the heat and simmer gently for 10 minutes until the sauce is thick.

3 Add the basil leaves, capers and a little salt and stir through for 1 minute. Serve with freshly cooked pasta, sprinkled with Parmesan, if liked.

serves **4**
preparation time **5 minutes**
cooking time **8 minutes**

Gorgonzola sauce

**25 g (1 oz) butter, plus extra
   to serve
250 g (8 oz) Gorgonzola
   cheese, crumbled
150 ml (¼ pint) double cream
2 tablespoons dry vermouth
1 teaspoon cornflour
2 tablespoons chopped sage
salt and pepper
sage leaves, to garnish**

1 Melt the butter in a heavy-based saucepan. Sprinkle in the Gorgonzola and stir it over a very gentle heat for 2–3 minutes until the cheese is melted.

2 Pour in the cream, vermouth and cornflour, whisking well to amalgamate. Stir in the sage. Cook, whisking all the time, until the sauce boils and thickens. Taste the sauce and season with salt and pepper

3 Pour the sauce over freshly cooked pasta and mix well. Garnish with sage leaves before serving.

PASTA TIP
Gorgonzola is a creamy yellow, semi-soft cheese, with characteristic blue-green veins and a rich, strong flavour. It was first produced over a thousand years ago in a village in the north of Italy called Gorgonzola, hence the name, and is one of the world's oldest cheeses. It can be eaten by itself or used in sauces, as here.

serves **4**
preparation time **5 minutes**
cooking time **5–7 minutes**

Clam ragu

1 teaspoon olive oil
1 small onion, finely chopped
1 garlic clove, crushed
1 red chilli, deseeded and
    finely chopped
1 kg (2 lb) clams in their shells,
    prepared
125 ml (4 fl oz) dry white wine
500 g (1 lb) tomatoes, skinned
    and mashed
handful of basil leaves, torn

1 Heat the oil in a large saucepan, add the onion, garlic and chilli and fry for 2 minutes.

2 Add the clams, wine and tomatoes, then cover and cook for 3–5 minutes until all the clams are opened, discarding any that remain closed.

3 Add freshly cooked pasta and the basil and stir well to combine before serving.

PASTA TIP
To peel tomatoes, put them in a bowl and cover with boiling water for 15 seconds, then lift out with a slotted spoon and plunge into cold water. Drain them and peel off the skins.

serves **4**
preparation time **10 minutes**
cooking time **25 minutes**

Vegetable ragoût

1 tablespoon olive oil
2 garlic cloves, crushed
1 onion, chopped
1 carrot, finely chopped
  and blanched
1 celery stick, chopped
1 red pepper, cored,
  deseeded and chopped
4 ripe plum tomatoes,
  chopped
3 tablespoons ready-made
  red pesto
salt and pepper
2 tablespoons chopped
  parsley, to garnish

1 Heat the oil in a saucepan, add the garlic and onion and fry for 3–5 minutes, until softened. Add the carrot and celery and fry for 5 minutes more. Stir in the red pepper, with plenty of salt and pepper. Fry for a further 10 minutes, adding a little water if necessary.

2 Add the tomatoes and pesto to the red pepper mixture. Cook for 5 minutes, then taste and add more salt and pepper if required.

3 Spoon the sauce over freshly cooked pasta, spinkled with pepper, and garnish with the chopped parsley.

serves **4**
preparation time **10 minutes**
cooking time **16–20 minutes**

Spicy sausage sauce

2 teaspoons cardamom pods
1 teaspoon cumin seeds
1 teaspoon fennel seeds
2 tablespoons olive oil
1 red onion, thinly sliced
500 g (1 lb) sausages, skins
   removed
50 g (2 oz) pine nuts
3 tablespoons chopped herbs,
   such as parsley, fennel and
   oregano
150 g (5 oz) green cabbage,
   very finely shredded
300 ml (½ pint) single cream
salt and pepper

1 Crush the cardamom pods using a pestle and mortar to release the seeds. Discard the shells and add the cumin and fennel seeds. Crush until lightly ground.

2 Heat the oil in a large heavy-based frying pan and fry the red onion for 3 minutes. Add the skinned sausages and fry gently, breaking the sausages up into small pieces with a wooden spoon, for 6–8 minutes until cooked through.

3 Add the pine nuts, herbs and crushed seeds to the pan and cook gently for 3–5 minutes, stirring frequently. Add the cabbage and fry for 2 minutes.

4 Pour in the cream and heat through for a further 2 minutes. Season with salt and pepper to taste and serve with freshly cooked pasta.

PASTA TIP
Packed with plenty of spices, this comforting sauce transforms even the dullest of sausages into a deliciously meaty pasta sauce. If you can get them, use sausages flavoured with apple, leek or mild spices, which will work really well. Failing that, ordinary lean sausages will be fine.

serves **4–6**
preparation time **15 minutes**
cooking time **5 minutes**

Walnut sauce

300 ml (½ pint) milk
2 slices wholemeal bread,
   crusts removed
300 g (10 oz) walnut pieces
1 garlic clove, crushed
50 g (2 oz) freshly grated
   Parmesan cheese, plus
   extra to garnish
100 ml (3½ fl oz) olive oil
150 ml (¼ pint) double cream
salt and pepper

1 Pour the milk into a shallow dish and soak the bread slices in it until all the milk has been absorbed.

2 Meanwhile, spread the walnuts on a baking sheet and toast in a preheated oven, 190°C (375°F), Gas Mark 5, for 5 minutes. Set aside to cool.

3 Put the bread, walnuts, garlic, Parmesan and olive oil into a food processor or blender and blend until smooth. Season to taste with salt and pepper, then stir in the double cream. Serve immediately tossed with freshly cooked pasta and garnished with freshly grated Parmesan.

serves **4**
preparation time **10 minutes**
cooking time **5 minutes**

Rocket and cherry tomato sauce

3 tablespoons olive oil
2 garlic cloves, finely
   chopped
500 g (1 lb) very ripe cherry
   tomatoes, halved
1 tablespoon balsamic
   vinegar
175 g (6 oz) rocket
salt and pepper
Parmesan cheese shavings,
   to serve

1 Heat the oil in a frying pan, add the garlic and cook for 1 minute until golden. Add the tomatoes and cook for barely 1 minute. The tomatoes should only just heat through and start to disintegrate.

2 Sprinkle the tomatoes with the balsamic vinegar, allow it to evaporate, then toss in the rocket. Carefully stir the rocket to mix it with the tomatoes and heat through so that it is just wilted. Season well with salt and plenty of freshly ground black pepper.

3 Serve immediately tossed with freshly cooked pasta and covered with plenty of Parmesan shavings.

serves **4**
preparation time **10 minutes**
cooking time **15 minutes**

Smoked salmon
and dill sauce

25 g (1 oz) butter
1 fennel bulb, finely chopped
2 small courgettes, diced
2 garlic cloves, crushed
100 ml (3½ fl oz) white wine
100 g (3½ oz) frozen peas
small handful of dill, chopped
250 g (8 oz) mascarpone
cheese
150 g (5 oz) smoked salmon,
cut into pieces
salt and pepper

1 Melt the butter in a large saucepan and fry the fennel and courgettes very gently for 6–8 minutes until softened but not browned. Add the garlic and fry for 2 minutes.

2 Add the wine and a little salt and pepper and bring to the boil. Let the sauce bubble for a minute until the wine is slightly reduced.

3 Transfer the sauce to a food processor or blender and blend very lightly until it is pulpy but not smooth.

4 Tip the sauce back into the pan and add the peas, dill, mascarpone and smoked salmon. Cook gently until heated through. Check the seasoning and serve with freshly cooked pasta.

PASTA TIP
This sauce provides a perfect use for packages of smoked salmon trimmings, which are very cheap but taste just as good as the more expensive choice pieces. Conveniently, the trimmings are also the right size for stirring into a delicious pasta sauce.

serves **2**
preparation time **5 minutes**
cooking time **10 minutes**

Smoked salmon
and asparagus sauce

175 g (6 oz) asparagus tips
125 g (4 oz) smoked salmon,
   cut into thin strips
300 ml (½ pint) double cream
1 tablespoon chopped
   tarragon
salt and pepper
Parmesan cheese shavings,
   to garnish (optional)

1 Blanch the asparagus tips in lightly salted boiling water for 5 minutes. Drain the tips under cold running water and pat dry.

2 Put the asparagus, smoked salmon, cream, tarragon and salt and pepper into a saucepan and warm gently until heated through.

3 Serve with freshly cooked pasta and garnish with wafer-thin shavings of Parmesan cheese, if liked.

serves **4**
preparation time **20 minutes**
cooking time **8–15 minutes**

Tomato curry sauce

1 tablespoon olive oil
1 onion, finely chopped
2 garlic cloves, crushed
1 tablespoon Madras curry
  powder
2 tablespoons tomato purée
400 g (13 oz) can chopped
  tomatoes
2 teaspoons garam masala
2 tablespoons chopped
  coriander leaves
coriander leaves, to garnish

1 Heat the oil in a frying pan, add the onion and garlic and fry for 3–5 minutes, until the onion has softened.

2 Stir in the curry powder, tomato purée and chopped tomatoes. Simmer the sauce, uncovered, for 5–10 minutes, then sprinkle in the garam masala, followed by the chopped coriander. Stir well.

3 Pile freshly cooked pasta in a heated bowl and drizzle with a little oil. Season with pepper. Pour over the sauce and toss lightly. Serve garnished with coriander leaves.

PASTA TIP
Spicy meatballs go very well with this sauce. Use lamb mince combined with grated onion, a little Parmesan, tomato purée and some chilli, coriander and cumin. Fry the meatballs in olive oil, then add them to the dish.

Salads

Sustaining and healthy, pasta makes the perfect base for fabulous salads. From sophisticated Warm Ravioli Salad with Beetroot and Bitter Leaves to simple Chicken and Avocado Salad, there's a dish for every occasion.

serves **4**
preparation time **5 minutes, plus cooling**
cooking time **8–12 minutes**

Italian salmon salad

250 g (8 oz) farfalle
200 g (7 oz) can salmon in
brine, drained and flaked
1 red pepper, cored, deseeded
and finely diced
½ cucumber, finely diced
12 pitted black olives
2 tablespoons mayonnaise
watercress sprigs, to garnish

1 Cook the pasta in a large saucepan of salted boiling water for 8–12 minutes, or according to packet instructions, until just tender. Drain thoroughly and leave to cool a little.

2 Mix the flaked salmon with the red pepper, cucumber, olives and pasta. Pour over the mayonnaise and toss lightly. Arrange in a serving dish and garnish with watercress sprigs.

serves **4**
preparation time **15 minutes, plus cooling**
cooking time **8–12 minutes**

Chicken
and avocado salad

250 g (8 oz) farfalle
½ tablespoon olive oil
250 g (8 oz) cooked chicken,
  cut into strips
2 celery sticks, finely sliced
10 pitted black olives
1 large ripe avocado, peeled,
  pitted and cubed
125 ml (4 fl oz) French
  dressing
snipped chives, to garnish

1 Cook the pasta in a large pan of salted boiling water for 8–12 minutes, or according to packet instructions, until just tender. Drain under cold water in a colander, drain again and transfer to a large salad bowl. Mix with the olive oil and leave to cool.

2 Mix the chicken, celery and olives into the cooled pasta in the serving bowl.

3 Mix the avocado with the French dressing in a separate bowl. Pour the avocado and dressing mixture over the pasta and toss lightly. Garnish with snipped chives before serving.

serves **4**
preparation time **8 minutes, plus standing**
cooking time **10 minutes**

Warm pasta salad

250 g (8 oz) malloreddus
250 g (8 oz) frozen peas,
thawed
6 tablespoons extra virgin
olive oil
6 spring onions, trimmed and
roughly chopped
2 garlic cloves, crushed
8 marinated artichoke hearts,
thickly sliced
4 tablespoons chopped mint
grated rind and juice of
½ lemon
salt and pepper

1 Cook the pasta in a saucepan of salted boiling water for about 6 minutes. Add the peas, bring back to the boil, and cook for a further 2–3 minutes until the peas and pasta are tender.

2 Meanwhile, heat 2 tablespoons of the oil in a frying pan and stir-fry the spring onions and garlic for 1–2 minutes until softened.

3 Drain the pasta, tip it into a bowl, then stir in the spring onions and garlic, artichoke hearts, mint and the remaining oil. Toss well, season with salt and pepper, then leave to rest for 10 minutes.

4 Stir in the lemon juice and serve the salad warm, garnished with lemon rind.

PASTA TIP
Malloreddus is a rice-shaped pasta available from larger supermarkets and specialist Italian food stores. It is often used in soups, but here it is combined with peas, marinated artichoke hearts, lemon and fresh herbs to make a deliciously fresh warm salad.

serves **4**
preparation time **20 minutes**
cooking time **8–12 minutes**

Winter macaroni salad

300 g (10 oz) macaroni
¼ medium white cabbage,
   shredded
1 onion, sliced into rings
2 carrots, cut into thin sticks
1 leek, finely sliced
250 g (8 oz) rindless back
   bacon, grilled and chopped
6 tablespoons mayonnaise
4 tablespoons milk
2 tablespoons tomato purée
salt and pepper
1 tablespoon chopped
   parsley, to garnish

1 Cook the pasta in a large saucepan of salted boiling water for 8–12 minutes, or according to packet instructions, until just tender.

2 Drain the pasta under cold water in a colander, drain again and transfer to a large salad bowl.

3 Add the cabbage, onion, carrots, leek and half the bacon to the salad bowl. Toss well with the pasta and add salt and pepper to taste.

4 Mix the mayonnaise and milk with the tomato purée in a bowl. Spoon over the salad and toss well. Garnish with chopped parsley and the remaining bacon and chill until required.

serves **4**
preparation time **30 minutes, plus standing and chilling**
cooking time **8–12 minutes**

Grilled pepper
and anchovy salad

**3 peppers (1 red, 1 green and
  1 yellow)**
250 g (8 oz) fusilli
**300 g (10 oz) can whole
  button mushrooms,
  drained**
**50 g (2 oz) can anchovies in
  oil, drained and roughly
  chopped**
salt and pepper
basil leaves, to garnish

dressing
**8 tablespoons hazelnut,
  walnut or olive oil**
**2 tablespoons raspberry or
  red wine vinegar**
**2 teaspoons wholegrain
  mustard**

1 Roast the peppers under a preheated hot grill for 10–12 minutes until the skins are black and blistered, turning them occasionally. Put the peppers in a bowl, cover it with clingfilm and leave them to cool.

2 Cook the pasta in a large pan of salted boiling water for 8–12 minutes, or according to packet instructions, until just tender.

3 Meanwhile, whisk together the dressing ingredients in a large bowl. Drain the pasta and refresh it briefly under cold water. Drain it again and add it to the bowl. Toss the pasta well to mix it with the dressing. Season to taste. Leave to cool, stirring occasionally.

4 Remove the peppers from the bowl and hold them under cold running water. Rub off the charred skins with your fingers then slit open the peppers and remove the cores and seeds. Dry them on kitchen paper, then cut the flesh lengthways into thin strips.

5 Combine the pepper strips and the liquid from the bowl with the cold pasta with the mushrooms and anchovies, tossing them together. Cover the bowl tightly and place in the refrigerator for 1–2 hours. Before serving, toss the salad again and garnish with the basil.

serves **4**
preparation time **10 minutes**
cooking time **12 minutes**

Warm ravioli salad
with beetroot and bitter leaves

4 tablespoons extra virgin olive oil
2 red onions, thinly sliced
2 garlic cloves, thinly sliced
500 g (1 lb) fresh spinach and ricotta ravioli
375 g (12 oz) cooked beetroot in natural juices, drained and diced
2 tablespoons capers in brine, drained and rinsed
2 tablespoons balsamic vinegar
a few mixed bitter salad leaves (such as chicory, radicchio, rocket and frisée)
parsley sprigs
basil leaves
salt
pecorino cheese shavings, to serve (optional)

1 Heat 1 tablespoon of the oil in a large pan and fry the onions and garlic over a medium heat for 10 minutes, until softened and golden.

2 Meanwhile, cook the ravioli in a large pan of salted boiling water for 3 minutes, until it is just tender. Drain and toss with the remaining oil.

3 Add the beetroot to the onions with the capers and vinegar and heat through. Stir the vegetables into the ravioli then transfer them to a large bowl to cool for 5 minutes, gathering in all the juices from the pan.

4 Arrange the ravioli in bowls or on plates with the salad leaves and herbs. Serve topped with pecorino shavings, if liked.

serves **4–6**
preparation time **20 minutes, plus marinating**
cooking time **5 minutes**

Marinated beef
and noodle salad

400 g (13 oz) rare roast beef, cut into thin strips

marinade
50 ml (2 fl oz) lemon juice
50 ml (2 fl oz) Thai fish sauce
2 tablespoons soy sauce
3 tablespoons dark brown sugar
2 teaspoons sambal oelek (bottled red chillies)

salad
300 g (10 oz) fresh wheat noodles
25 g (1 oz) mint leaves, roughly chopped
25 g (1 oz) coriander leaves, roughly chopped
1 round lettuce, torn into pieces
1 cucumber, peeled, deseeded and sliced
1 red onion, sliced
1 radicchio, torn into pieces

1 Place the beef in a shallow dish. Combine the marinade ingredients and pour the marinade over the beef. Cover and leave to marinate for 2 hours.

2 Cook the noodles in a large saucepan of salted boiling water for 8–12 minutes, or according to packet instructions, until just tender. Drain well. While still hot, add the mint and coriander, tossing until well combined.

3 Arrange the lettuce, cucumber, onion and radicchio on a serving plate and add the noodles.

4 Arrange the meat slices on top of the salad and pour over any marinade remaining in the dish.

> **PASTA TIP**
> *Nam pla* (Thai fish sauce), literally means 'fish water'. It is a clear, amber-coloured seasoning sauce with a pungent, salty flavour. It is used in Thai and Vietnamese cooking to bring out the flavour of other foods. Vietnamese *nuoc mam* is darker in colour and has a stronger fishy taste than *nam pla*.

Baked

There's nothing like a bubbling, golden lasagne or hearty pasta bake for comfort food. If it's a spicy option you're after, try Mexican Chilli Shell Bake, but for some good old-fashioned indulgence, enjoy creamy Macaroni Cheese.

serves **6**
preparation time **30 minutes**
cooking time **about 1 hour**

Lasagne al forno

200 g (7 oz) no pre-cook
   lasagne sheets
pepper

meat sauce
2 aubergines, peeled
   and diced
2 red onions, chopped
2 garlic cloves, crushed
300 ml (½ pint) vegetable
   stock
4 tablespoons red wine
500 g (1 lb) lean beef mince
2 x 400 g (13 oz) cans
   chopped tomatoes

cheese sauce
50 g (2 oz) butter
50 g (2 oz) plain flour
600 ml (1 pint) milk
6 tablespoons freshly grated
   Parmesan cheese

1 To make the meat sauce place the aubergines, onions, garlic, stock and wine in a large nonstick saucepan. Cover and simmer briskly for 5 minutes.

2 Remove the lid and cook for about 5 minutes more until the aubergine is tender and the liquid is absorbed, adding a little more stock if necessary. Remove the pan from the heat, allow the sauce to cool slightly, then purée in a food processor or blender.

3 Brown the mince in a nonstick frying pan. Add the aubergine mixture, tomatoes and pepper to taste. Simmer briskly, uncovered, for about 10 minutes until thickened.

4 Meanwhile, make the cheese sauce. Melt the butter in a heavy-based saucepan, stir in the flour and cook for 1 minute. Remove the pan from the heat and gradually add the milk, whisking continually until it is all combined. Return to the heat and stir until bubbling. Leave to cook for 2 minutes, stirring, then remove from the heat. Add 4 tablespoons of the Parmesan, stir to combine, and season to taste with pepper.

5 Assemble the lasagne in a 1.8 litre (3 pint) ovenproof dish by alternating layers of meat sauce, lasagne and cheese sauce, starting with meat sauce and finishing with cheese sauce. Sprinkle with the remaining Parmesan. Bake in a preheated oven, 180°C (350°F), Gas Mark 4, for 30–40 minutes until browned.

serves **4**
preparation time **20 minutes**
cooking time **1 hour**

Lamb
and pasta bake

250 g (8 oz) **macaroni**
1 **onion, thinly sliced**
375 g (12 oz) **cooked lean
  lamb, cubed**
400 g (13 oz) **can chopped
  tomatoes**
4 tablespoons **tomato purée**
2 tablespoons **mixed
  dried herbs**
400 g (13 oz) **can red kidney
  beans, drained**
1 teaspoon **cornflour**
1 tablespoon **water**
salt and pepper

topping
75 g (3 oz) **Cheddar cheese,
  grated**
75 g (3 oz) **wholemeal
  breadcrumbs**

1 Grease the base and sides of a 1.8 litre (3 pint) ovenproof dish. Cook the pasta in a large saucepan of salted boiling water for 8–12 minutes, or according to packet instructions, until just tender.

2 Meanwhile, dry-fry the onion in a nonstick frying pan for 3 minutes, until softened.

3 Transfer the onion to a bowl and mix in the lamb, tomatoes, tomato purée, mixed herbs and kidney beans.

4 Drain the pasta well. In a cup, mix the cornflour and water to form a smooth paste. Stir the paste into the meat mixture with the cooked pasta. Season to taste with salt and pepper.

5 Spoon the lamb mixture into the prepared dish. Mix together the grated cheese and breadcrumbs and sprinkle over the top.

6 Bake the pasta in a preheated oven, 200°C (400°F), Gas Mark 6, for 45 minutes, covering the dish with foil after 30 minutes if the topping starts to over-brown.

serves **4**
preparation time **12 minutes**
cooking time **16 minutes**

Quick mushroom
and spinach lasagne

12 fresh lasagne sheets
3 tablespoons extra virgin
olive oil
500 g (1 lb) mixed mushrooms
(such as shiitake, oyster and
chestnut), sliced
200 g (7 oz) mascarpone
cheese
150 g (5 oz) taleggio cheese,
derinded and cubed
125 g (4 oz) baby spinach
salt and pepper

1 Place the lasagne sheets in a large roasting tin and cover with boiling water. Leave to stand for 5 minutes, or until tender, then drain off the water.

2 Heat the oil in a large frying pan and fry the mushrooms for 5 minutes. Add the mascarpone and turn up the heat. Cook for another 1 minute until the sauce is thick. Season with salt and pepper.

3 Grease the base and sides of a 1.8 litre (3 pint) ovenproof dish and place 3 sheets of lasagne on it, slightly overlapping. Top with a little of the taleggio, one-third of the mushroom sauce and one-third of the spinach. Repeat with two more layers, then top the final layer of lasagne with the remaining taleggio.

4 Cook the lasagne under a hot grill for 5 minutes until the cheese is golden.

PASTA TIP
Whoever said lasagne had to be complicated? Throw this dish together for a simple supper that vegetarians and meat-eaters alike will love. Use whatever mushrooms you have – shiitake add a good earthy flavour, but chestnut mushrooms are also good.

serves **4**
preparation time **15 minutes**
cooking time **45–60 minutes**

Classic cannelloni

8 no pre-cook lasagne sheets
25 g (1 oz) freshly grated
Parmesan cheese
15 g (½ oz) butter

filling
2 tablespoons olive oil
50 g (2 oz) chopped onions
1 garlic clove, crushed
250 g (8 oz) finely minced beef
2 tomatoes, skinned,
deseeded and chopped
1 tablespoon fine fresh
breadcrumbs
25 g (1 oz) freshly grated
Parmesan cheese
¼ teaspoon dried marjoram
1 egg, lightly beaten
salt and pepper

sauce
300 ml (½ pint) milk
150 ml (¼ pint) single cream
40 g (1½ oz) butter
40 g (1½ oz) flour
grated nutmeg
salt and pepper

1 To make the filling, heat the oil in a heavy-based saucepan, add the onions and garlic and sauté for 5 minutes until soft. Add the minced beef and cook, stirring, until browned. Add the tomatoes, cover and cook for 10 minutes over a low heat. Remove the pan from the heat and stir in the breadcrumbs, Parmesan, marjoram, egg and salt and pepper to taste. Set aside to cool.

2 Cook the lasagne in a large saucepan of salted boiling water for 8–12 minutes, or according to packet instructions, until just tender.

3 Meanwhile, make the sauce by heating the milk and cream gently in a saucepan. Melt the butter in another saucepan and stir in the flour. Cook gently over a low heat for 1 minute, stirring well. Remove from the heat and whisk in the hot milk and cream. Return to the heat and bring to the boil while whisking until thick and smooth. Season with salt, pepper and nutmeg to taste. Cover and keep warm.

4 Grease the base and sides of a 1.8 litre (3 pint) ovenproof dish. Remove the lasagne with a slotted spoon and drain well. Spoon one-eighth of the filling down one long side of each sheet of lasagne. Roll up each one into a cylinder. Arrange the cylinders side by side in the prepared dish.

5 Spoon the sauce over the pasta. Sprinkle with Parmesan, dot with butter and bake in a preheated oven, 190°C (375°F), Gas Mark 5, for 20–30 minutes until bubbling and golden.

serves **4–6**
preparation time **20 minutes, plus cooling**
cooking time **45–60 minutes**

Cannelloni
with spinach

750 g (1½ lb) fresh spinach
50 g (2 oz) butter
250 g (8 oz) ricotta or cottage
cheese, sieved
75 g (3 oz) freshly grated
Parmesan cheese
pinch of grated nutmeg
2 large eggs
12 cannelloni tubes
25 g (1 oz) flour
300 ml (½ pint) milk
4 tablespoons bran cereal
salt and pepper

1 Place the spinach in a large pan with a little water and cook, covered, over a medium heat, shaking the pan occasionally, for 3–4 minutes until just wilted. Drain in a colander, pressing out all the moisture, then chop finely.

2 Melt half of the butter in a saucepan, add the spinach and stir well. Remove the pan from the heat. Beat the ricotta or cottage cheese and half of the Parmesan into the spinach and season with salt, pepper and nutmeg. Beat in the eggs. Set aside to cool.

3 Cook the cannelloni tubes in a pan of salted boiling water for 8–12 minutes, or according to packet instructions, until just tender. Drain, refresh in cold water, and drain again. Dry thoroughly with kitchen paper. Set aside to cool.

4 Melt the remaining butter in a pan, stir in the flour and cook for 1 minute. Remove from the heat and gradually stir in the milk, stirring constantly. Bring to the boil, season with salt and pepper, and simmer for 5 minutes. Taste and adjust the seasoning if necessary.

5 Grease the base and sides of a 1.8 litre (3 pint) ovenproof dish. Spoon the spinach filling into the cannelloni tubes and place them in the dish. Pour the sauce over and sprinkle with the remaining Parmesan mixed with the bran cereal.

6 Bake in a preheated oven, 180°C (350°F), Gas Mark 4, for 35–40 minutes or until the topping is brown and crusty.

serves **4**
preparation time **25 minutes, plus standing**
cooking time **40 minutes**

Chicken
and macaroni bake

250 g (8 oz) macaroni
2 tablespoons sunflower oil
4 chicken breast fillets, about
400 g (13 oz) in total, thickly
sliced
1 onion, finely chopped
1 garlic clove, crushed
1 large red dessert apple,
chopped
salt and pepper
sage leaves or chopped
parsley, to garnish
(optional)

cheese sauce
350 ml (12 fl oz) milk
1 small onion, sliced
6 whole black peppercorns
1 bay leaf
40 g (1½ oz) butter
40 g (1½ oz) plain flour
125 g (4 oz) mature Cheddar
cheese, grated
pinch of grated nutmeg

1 Grease a 1.8 litre (3 pint) ovenproof dish. To make the sauce, put the milk, onion, peppercorns and bay leaf in a saucepan and bring slowly to the boil. As soon as the liquid starts to bubble, remove from the heat, cover and set aside to infuse for 30 minutes.

2 Meanwhile, cook the pasta in a saucepan of salted boiling water for 8–12 minutes, or according to packet instructions, until just tender.

3 While the pasta is cooking, heat the oil in a large frying pan over a medium heat. Add the chicken and brown on all sides, stirring constantly, for 3 minutes. Lower the heat, add the onion and garlic and cook for 5 minutes or until the onion is soft. Remove from the heat.

4 Drain the pasta, then stir it into the chicken mixture with the apple and salt and pepper to taste. Set aside.

5 Strain the infused milk through a fine sieve set over a measuring jug. Discard the solids in the sieve.

6 Melt the butter in a heavy-based saucepan over a medium heat. Stir in the flour and cook for 1 minute. Remove from the heat and gradually stir in the infused milk. Return to the heat and bring to the boil, stirring constantly.

7 Reserve a quarter of the cheese and stir the rest into the sauce, with the nutmeg and salt and pepper to taste. When the cheese has melted, remove the saucepan from the heat and pour the sauce over the reserved chicken mixture and mix thoroughly. Transfer to the prepared dish and sprinkle with the reserved cheese.

8 Bake in the centre of a preheated oven, 200°C (400°F), Gas Mark 6, for 25 minutes or until the top is golden brown. Garnish with sage leaves or parsley, if wished.

serves **4**
preparation time **45 minutes**
cooking time **55 minutes**

Mexican chilli shell bake

1 tablespoon olive oil
1 onion, finely chopped
2 garlic cloves, crushed
1 green chilli, deseeded
 and chopped
250 g (8 oz) minced lean beef
2 teaspoons mild chilli
 powder
3 tablespoons tomato purée
250 g (8 oz) conchiglie
150 g (5 oz) mozzarella
 cheese, grated
75 g (3 oz) Cheddar cheese,
 grated
2 eggs, beaten
salt and pepper

1 Lightly grease a 1.8 litre (3 pint) ovenproof dish. Heat the oil in a heavy-based saucepan. Add the onion and garlic and fry for about 5 minutes, stirring occasionally until softened.

2 Add the chilli and minced beef. Fry for 5 minutes, stirring constantly. Stir in the chilli powder and the tomato purée, with salt and pepper to taste. Simmer, partially covered, for about 25 minutes to form a dry spicy sauce.

3 Meanwhile, cook the pasta in a large pan of salted boiling water for 8–12 minutes, or according to packet instructions, until just tender. Drain the pasta and transfer it to the prepared dish. Pour the sauce over the pasta and mix well.

4 Mix the two cheeses with the beaten eggs in a bowl, then pour the mixture over the pasta. Bake in a preheated oven, 190°C (375°F), Gas Mark 5, for 20 minutes. Serve at once.

serves **4**
preparation time **10 minutes**
cooking time about **40 minutes**

Tuna penne bake

300 g (10 oz) penne
1 tablespoon olive oil
1 onion, chopped
150 ml (¼ pint) passata
1 tablespoon mixed dried herbs
200 g (7 oz) can tuna in brine, drained
175 g (6 oz) Cheddar cheese, grated
50 g (2 oz) pitted black olives, halved
salt
herb sprigs, to garnish

to serve
crisp green salad
ciabatta or focaccia

1 Lightly grease a 1.8 litre (3 pint) ovenproof dish.

2 Cook the pasta in a large pan of salted boiling water for 8–12 minutes, or according to packet instructions, until just tender.

3 Meanwhile, heat the oil in a heavy-based saucepan. Fry the onion for 3–5 minutes, stirring constantly until softened. Stir in the passata and mixed herbs, bring back to the boil and simmer for 5 minutes.

4 Drain the pasta and place it in the prepared dish. Flake the tuna over the pasta. Pour the tomato sauce over the tuna and sprinkle the grated Cheddar cheese on top. Scatter the olives over the cheese.

5 Bake in a preheated oven, 180°C (350°F), Gas Mark 4, for 30 minutes. Garnish with herb sprigs and serve at once with a crisp green salad and some ciabatta or focaccia.

PASTA TIP
Passata, or sieved tomatoes, is a useful store-cupboard ingredient that can be used in many pasta sauces. Its smooth consistency and lack of pips make it preferable to canned chopped tomatoes in some recipes.

serves **4**
preparation time **15 minutes**
cooking time **18–25 minutes**

Macaroni cheese

375 g (12 oz) macaroni
2 tablespoons olive oil
1 onion, finely chopped
2 garlic cloves, crushed
2 teaspoons chopped
   rosemary
125 g (4 oz) bacon, diced
   (optional)
200 ml (7 fl oz) single cream
200 ml (7 fl oz) milk
200 g (7 oz) Cheddar cheese,
   grated
salt and pepper
crisp green salad, to serve
   (optional)

1 Cook the pasta in a large saucepan of salted boiling water for 8–12 minutes, or according to packet instructions, until just tender.

2 Meanwhile, heat the oil in a large saucepan and gently fry the onion, garlic, rosemary and bacon, if using, for 5 minutes until softened.

3 Add the cream and milk, bring to boiling point, then remove from the heat and stir in two-thirds of the cheese. Season with salt and pepper.

4 Drain the pasta well and stir it into the cheese sauce. Divide the mixture between 4 small ovenproof dishes. Scatter over the remaining cheese and bake in a preheated oven, 230°C (450°F), Gas Mark 8, for 10–12 minutes until bubbling and golden. Cool slightly, before serving with a crisp green salad, if liked.

Meat

Smoky bacon, spicy sausage, zesty lemon chicken and chunky meatballs all make perfect partners for pasta. Try Linguine with Peas and Pancetta for a simple family supper, or impress dinner guests with Conchiglie with Rich Rabbit Sauce.

serves **6**
preparation time **20 minutes**
cooking time **1 hour 20 minutes**

Italian meatballs

**2 slices of stale bread, crusts
    removed**
75 ml (3 fl oz) milk
4 tablespoons olive oil
**6 spring onions or 1 small
    onion, chopped**
1 garlic clove, chopped
750 g (1½ lb) lean minced beef
**2 tablespoons freshly grated
    Parmesan cheese**
1 teaspoon grated nutmeg
300 ml (½ pint) dry white wine
**400 g (13 oz) can chopped
    tomatoes**
2 bay leaves
500 g (1 lb) tagliatelle
25 g (1 oz) butter
salt and pepper
basil leaves, to garnish

1 Put the bread into a large bowl, moisten with the milk and leave to soak.

2 Heat half the oil and fry the onions and garlic for 5 minutes until soft and just beginning to brown.

3 Combine the meat with the moistened bread. Add the cooked onion and garlic, the Parmesan, nutmeg and salt and pepper. Work together with your hands until the mixture is well mixed and smooth.

4 With clean wet hands, roll the mixture into 30 even-sized balls. Heat the remaining oil in a large nonstick frying pan and brown the meatballs in batches, then transfer them to a shallow ovenproof dish.

5 Pour the wine and tomatoes into the frying pan and bring to the boil, scraping up any sediment from the bottom of the pan. Add the bay leaves, season with salt and pepper and boil rapidly for 5 minutes.

6 Pour the sauce over the meatballs, cover with foil and bake in a preheated oven, 180°C (350°F), Gas Mark 4, for 1 hour or until tender.

7 Shortly before serving cook the pasta in a large saucepan of salted boiling water for 8–12 minutes, or according to packet instructions, until tender. Drain and toss with butter, then serve with the meatballs garnished with basil leaves.

serves **4**
preparation time **5 minutes**
cooking time **8–12 minutes**

Penne with chorizo,
borlotti beans and peppers

375 g (12 oz) penne
125 g (4 oz) small chorizo
sausages, thinly sliced
400 g (13 oz) can borlotti
beans, rinsed and drained
300 g (10 oz) chargrilled
peppers in oil, drained and
sliced
75 ml (3 fl oz) white wine
small handful of basil leaves,
torn into pieces
salt
freshly grated Parmesan
cheese, to serve

1 Cook the pasta in a large pan of salted boiling water for 8–12 minutes, or according to packet instructions, until just tender.

2 Meanwhile, fry the chorizo in a frying pan over a medium heat for 20 seconds on each side until crisp. Add the beans and stir until coated in the chorizo oil. Add the peppers and wine. Simmer for 2 minutes until the wine has reduced by half.

3 Drain the pasta well, then toss the chorizo and beans with the hot pasta and the basil. Season with salt and serve with freshly grated Parmesan.

PASTA TIP
This is a great standby dish that can be simply thrown together when you have not had the time to shop. Peppers in oil and chorizo keep really well in the refrigerator, so it's always well worth having a regular supply for an impromptu meal such as this one.

serves **4**
preparation time **5 minutes**
cooking time **20 minutes**

Lemony bean
and bacon penne

250 g (8 oz) penne
4 tablespoons olive oil
200 g (7 oz) back bacon,
chopped
2 onions, chopped
200 g (7 oz) cooked soya
beans
4 teaspoons chopped
rosemary
4 tablespoons lemon juice
50 g (2 oz) butter
salt and pepper

1 Cook the pasta in a large pan of salted boiling water for 8–12 minutes, or according to packet instructions, until just tender.

2 Meanwhile, heat the oil in a large frying pan and fry the bacon and onions for about 6–8 minutes, until golden.

3 Mix the lemon juice and butter in the pan. Season the sauce with salt and pepper and heat gently, stirring, until the butter has melted.

4 Lightly mash the soya beans in a bowl with the lemony butter juices, then add to the bacon and onions with the rosemary and cook gently for 2 minutes until the mixture is heated right through. Drain the pasta, add it to the pan and mix thoroughly.

serves **4**
preparation time **10 minutes**
cooking time **8–12 minutes**

Tagliatelle
with bacon, mushrooms and pine nuts

375 g (12 oz) green and white
   tagliatelle
25 g (1 oz) pine nuts
1 tablespoon olive oil
1 yellow pepper, cored,
   deseeded and chopped
2 teaspoons garlic purée,
   or crushed garlic
125 g (4 oz) button
   mushrooms, sliced
125 g (4 oz) rindless lean back
   bacon, grilled and cut into
   thin strips
1 tablespoon chopped parsley
500 g (1 lb) natural fromage
   frais or yogurt
pepper

to serve
Italian-style salad
ciabatta

1 Cook the pasta in a saucepan of salted boiling water for 8–12 minutes, or according to packet instructions, until just tender.

2 Meanwhile, heat a nonstick frying pan, add the pine nuts and toast them over a medium heat, stirring all the time, for 1–2 minutes until lightly brown. Remove the pine nuts and leave to cool, then heat the oil in the frying pan, add the pepper and cook for 2–3 minutes. Stir in the garlic, mushrooms, bacon, parsley and pepper to taste.

3 Reduce the heat and stir in the fromage frais or yogurt. Heat through very gently.

4 Drain the pasta and toss with the sauce. Sprinkle with the pine nuts before serving. Serve with an Italian-style salad and fresh ciabatta.

serves **4**
preparation time **5 minutes**
cooking time **8–12 minutes**

Linguine
with peas and pancetta

300 g (10 oz) linguine
2 tablespoons olive oil
150 g (6 oz) pancetta, diced
200 g (7 oz) frozen petit pois
8 tablespoons single cream
6 teaspoons ready-made
pesto
Parmesan cheese shavings
salt and pepper
basil leaves, to garnish
(optional)

1 Cook the pasta in a large pan of salted boiling water for 8–12 minutes, or according to packet instructions, until just tender.

2 Meanwhile, heat the oil in a frying pan, add the pancetta and fry for 4–5 minutes, stirring, until browned. Add the peas and cook for 2 minutes, then stir in the cream, pesto and salt and pepper and cook for 1 minute.

3 Drain the pasta, add to the frying pan and toss with the sauce. Spoon into shallow bowls and sprinkle with Parmesan and basil leaves, if liked.

PASTA TIP
Pancetta is an Italian cured bacon that is now readily available, usually diced, in supermarkets alongside the pre-packed ham and salami. If you can't find it, then use diced streaky or back bacon instead.

serves **4–6**
preparation time **5 minutes**
cooking time **about 30 minutes**

Pasta arrabiata
with mollica

3 tablespoons olive oil
2 shallots, finely chopped
8 slices of unsmoked
pancetta, chopped
2 teaspoons dried crushed
chillies
400 g (13 oz) can chopped
tomatoes
500–750 g (1–1½ lb) conchiglie
salt and pepper
parsley sprigs, to garnish

mollica
6 slices of white bread, crusts
removed
125 g (4 oz) butter
2 garlic cloves, finely chopped

1 Heat the oil in a saucepan and fry the shallots and pancetta gently for 6–8 minutes until golden. Add the chillies and chopped tomatoes, half cover the pan and simmer for 20 minutes until the sauce is thick and has reduced. Season to taste with salt and pepper.

2 Meanwhile, cook the pasta in a large saucepan of salted boiling water for 8–12 minutes, or according to packet instructions, until just tender.

3 To make the *mollica*, put the bread in a food processor or blender and reduce to crumbs. Heat the butter in a frying pan, add the garlic and breadcrumbs and stir-fry until golden and crisp. (Don't let the crumbs catch and burn or the dish will be ruined.)

4 Drain the pasta well, toss it with the tomato sauce and sprinkle each serving with some of the garlic crumbs. Garnish with parsley sprigs.

PASTA TIP
This is a hot and spicy sauce with the added crunch of golden fried breadcrumbs, which are called *mollica* or, more accurately, *mollica fritta*. *Mollica* is the Sicilian word for breadcrumbs. You can even toss plain pasta in the crumbs for a simple meal.

serves **4**
preparation time **10 minutes**
cooking time **15 minutes**

Lemon chicken pasta

375 g (12 oz) farfalle
1 teaspoon olive oil
1 onion, sliced
1 garlic clove, finely sliced
2 large cooked chicken
**   breasts, about 150 g (5 oz)**
**   each, shredded**
grated rind and juice of
**   2 lemons**
6 tablespoons crème fraîche
2 tablespoons chopped
**   parsley**
pepper
watercress and rocket salad,
**   to serve**

1 Cook the pasta in a large pan of salted boiling water for 8–12 minutes, or according to packet instructions, until just tender.

2 Meanwhile, heat the oil in a frying pan, add the onion and garlic and cook for 4–5 minutes until softened and beginning to turn golden.

3 Add the remaining ingredients and heat through. Drain the pasta and toss with the chicken mixture. Serve with a watercress and rocket salad.

PASTA TIP
This dish is delicious served with a watercress and rocket salad. Simply toss the watercress and salad leaves with a little olive oil and season with pepper.

serves **4**
preparation time **10 minutes**
cooking time **2 hours**

Conchiglie
with rich rabbit sauce

1 teaspoon olive oil
1 onion, chopped
1 carrot, finely chopped
1 celery stick, diced
1 rabbit, jointed, or
    4 chicken joints
1 teaspoon five-spice powder
1 tablespoon plain flour
pared rind of 1 orange
1 sprig rosemary
1 teaspoon chopped fresh
    marjoram
300 ml (½ pint) red wine
300 ml (½ pint) beef stock
375 g (12 oz) conchiglie
4 tablespoons crème fraîche
pepper
green salad, to serve

1 Heat the oil in a large saucepan, add the onion, carrot and celery and fry for 2–3 minutes until softened. Add the rabbit pieces and continue to fry for 2–3 minutes until browned all over, then add the spice and flour and stir to combine.

2 Add the orange rind, rosemary and marjoram, then gradually stir in the wine and stock. Bring the mixture to the boil then cover and simmer for about 2 hours until the rabbit is very tender. Carefully remove all the bones.

3 Towards the end of the cooking time, cook the pasta in a large saucepan of salted boiling water for 8–12 minutes, or according to packet instructions, until just tender, then drain. Add the rabbit, sauce and crème fraîche to the pasta and stir to combine, then serve with a green salad.

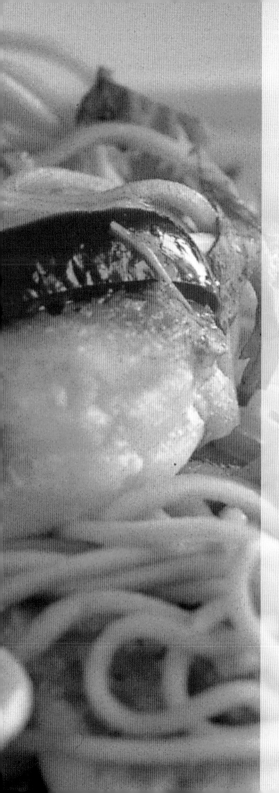

Fish and seafood

Delicately flavoured fish and shellfish are perfect for serving with pasta. Juicy pink salmon, salty anchovies, tender prawns and meaty monkfish all combine with fabulously flavoured sauces and pasta to make wonderful meals.

serves **4**
preparation time **10 minutes**
cooking time **about 15 minutes**

Salmon
with pesto and pasta

325 g (11 oz) **penne**
2 tablespoons **olive oil**
1 **onion, thinly sliced**
150 g (5 oz) **frozen peas**
2 tablespoons **ready-made pesto**
1 tablespoon **lemon juice**
25 g (1 oz) **freshly grated Parmesan cheese**
400 g (13 oz) **can red or pink salmon, drained, skin and bones removed**
salt and pepper
Parmesan cheese shavings, to garnish
leafy salad, to serve (optional)

1 Cook the pasta in a large saucepan of salted boiling water for 8–12 minutes, or according to packet instructions, until just tender.

2 Meanwhile, heat the oil in a frying pan, add the onion and fry for about 5 minutes until softened.

3 Add the peas to the pasta for the last 3 minutes of cooking time. Drain the pasta and peas, retaining a few tablespoons of the cooking water, and return to the pan.

4 Stir in the pesto, lemon juice, Parmesan, onion and reserved cooking water, and flake the salmon into the mixture. Season lightly with salt and pepper and toss gently. Serve immediately, topped with Parmesan shavings and accompanied by a leafy salad, if liked.

PASTA TIP
Canned salmon might not taste as good as its fresh counterpart, but it's ideal for creating an easy meal in minutes. Bottled pesto sauce is another valuable storecupboard standby. For this recipe, use either the familiar green pesto (made from basil and Parmesan) or the less well-known red pesto (flavoured with peppers and tomatoes).

serves **4**
preparation time **30 minutes**
cooking time **10–15 minutes**

Pasta
with broccoli and anchovies

4 tablespoons olive oil

25 g (1 oz) fresh white
breadcrumbs

500 g (1 lb) broccoli, broken
into small florets

375 g (12 oz) fusilli

2 garlic cloves, sliced

2 teaspoons grated
lemon rind

1 dried red chilli, deseeded
and chopped

50 g (2 oz) can anchovies in
oil, drained and chopped

50 g (2 oz) sultanas

2 tablespoons chopped
parsley

salt and pepper

freshly grated Parmesan
cheese, to serve (optional)

1 Heat 1 tablespoon of the oil in a small frying pan and stir-fry the breadcrumbs for 1–2 minutes until golden. Drain on kitchen paper and set aside.

2 Cook the broccoli for 1 minute in a large saucepan of salted boiling water. Drain, reserving the water, and immediately plunge the broccoli into cold water. Drain the broccoli, pat dry and set aside.

3 Pour the reserved water back into the pan, top up with more water and salt as necessary and bring back to the boil. Cook the pasta for 8–12 minutes, or according to packet instructions, until tender.

4 Meanwhile, heat 2 tablespoons of the remaining olive oil in a large frying pan and add the garlic, lemon rind, chilli, anchovies, sultanas and chopped parsley. Stir-fry the mixture for 3–4 minutes, or until softened.

5 Add the broccoli florets to the pan and fry for 2–3 minutes, until the broccoli is heated through and tender. Season with pepper to taste.

6 Drain the cooked pasta, shaking well to remove excess water. Return to the pan, toss with the remaining oil and then stir in the broccoli mixture. Taste and adjust the seasoning, if necessary. Serve at once, topped with the fried breadcrumbs and a little freshly grated Parmesan, if liked.

serves **4**
preparation time **10 minutes**
cooking time **8–12 minutes**

Spaghetti
with roasted asparagus and anchovies

375 g (12 oz) spaghetti
375 g (12 oz) asparagus,
   trimmed and cut into 7 cm
   (3 inch) lengths
5 tablespoons olive oil
50 g (2 oz) butter
½ teaspoon dried crushed
   chillies
2 garlic cloves, sliced
50 g (2 oz) anchovy fillets in
   oil, drained and chopped
2 tablespoons lemon juice
75 g (3 oz) Parmesan cheese
   shavings
salt

1 Cook the pasta in a large saucepan of salted boiling water for 8–12 minutes, or according to packet instructions, until just tender.

2 Meanwhile, place the asparagus in a roasting tin, drizzle with olive oil and dot with butter. Scatter with dried crushed chillies, garlic and anchovies and cook in a preheated oven, 200°C (400°F), Gas Mark 6, for 8 minutes until tender.

3 Drain the pasta well, toss it with the asparagus and squeeze over the lemon juice. Scatter the Parmesan over the top, season with salt and serve immediately.

PASTA TIP
Make this simple, flavoursome dish when asparagus is in season and at its best. The anchovies simply 'dissolve' during cooking and impart a wonderfully subtle saltiness.

serves **4**
preparation time **20 minutes**
cooking time **11–17 minutes**

Tagliatelle
with salmon

25 g (1 oz) butter
1 garlic clove, crushed
1 onion, chopped
425 g (14 oz) tagliatelle
250 g (8 oz) assorted
    mushrooms, sliced if large
250 g (8 oz) salmon fillet,
    cubed
2 tablespoons snipped chives
1 tablespoon chopped parsley
150 ml (¼ pint) double cream
salt and pepper
parsley sprigs, to garnish

to serve
green salad
French bread

1 Melt the butter in a frying pan. Add the garlic and onion and fry for 3–5 minutes, until softened but not browned.

2 Cook the pasta in a large saucepan of salted boiling water for 8–12 minutes, or according to packet instructions, until just tender.

3 Meanwhile, add the mushrooms to the frying pan and fry for 4 minutes, or until the mushrooms have softened. Reduce the heat and add the salmon. Cook for about 4 minutes, or until the fish is beginning to flake. Stir in the chives, parsley and cream. Season to taste with salt and pepper.

4 Drain the pasta and return it to the clean saucepan. Add the sauce, stirring carefully until well mixed. Garnish with parsley sprigs and serve immediately with a green salad and French bread.

serves **4**
preparation time **10 minutes**
cooking time **about 15 minutes**

Fusilli
with anchovies and olives

375 g (12 oz) fusilli
25 g (1 oz) butter
6 anchovy fillets, chopped
1 tablespoon tomato purée
1 tablespoon olive paste
6 pitted black olives, chopped
handful of basil leaves, torn
  into pieces
salt and pepper
freshly grated Parmesan
  cheese, to serve

1 Cook the pasta in a large saucepan of salted boiling water for 8–12 minutes, or according to packet instructions, until just tender.

2 Meanwhile, melt the butter in a large saucepan. Add the anchovy fillets, tomato purée, olive paste and olives. Stir over the heat until the mixture sizzles. Season well with pepper. Leave to cool for 1 minute.

3 Drain the pasta, add it to the saucepan and toss well. Add the basil leaves to the pasta. Serve immediately with freshly grated Parmesan.

serves **4**
preparation time **15 minutes**
cooking time **8–12 minutes**

Pasta
with spinach and anchovies

500 g (1 lb) vermicelli or spaghetti
1 kg (2 lb) fresh spinach, washed, or 625 g (1¼ lb) frozen leaf spinach
4 tablespoons olive oil
3 tablespoons pine nuts
2 garlic cloves, crushed
6 canned anchovies in oil, drained and chopped
3 tablespoons sultanas (optional)
melted butter
salt
freshly grated Parmesan cheese, to serve

1 Cook the pasta in a large saucepan of salted boiling water for 8–12 minutes, or according to packet instructions, until just tender.

2 Meanwhile, if using fresh spinach, place it in a large saucepan with just the water that clings to the leaves. Cook, covered, over a medium heat, shaking the pan occasionally, for 3–4 minutes until the spinach is just wilted and still bright green. Drain in a colander, pressing out all the moisture, then chop finely. If using frozen spinach, cook it according to the packet instructions.

3 Heat the oil in a saucepan and fry the pine nuts until golden. Remove with a slotted spoon and drain on kitchen paper. Add the garlic to the oil in the pan and fry until golden. Add the anchovies, stir in the spinach and cook for 2–3 minutes or until heated through. Stir in the pine nuts and the sultanas, if using.

4 Drain the pasta, toss it in a little melted butter and turn into a warmed serving bowl. Top with the sauce and fork through roughly. Serve with plenty of freshly grated Parmesan.

serves **4**
preparation time **10 minutes**
cooking time **10–14 minutes**

Garlicky prawns
with basil

375 g (12 oz) **fusilli**
25 g (1 oz) **pine nuts**
6 tablespoons **olive oil**
2 **garlic cloves, crushed**
pinch of **dried crushed chillies**
375 g (12 oz) **cooked peeled**
    tiger prawns
juice of ½ **lemon**
25 g (1 oz) **chopped basil**
    leaves
salt and pepper

1 Cook the pasta in a large saucepan of salted boiling water for 8–12 minutes, or according to packet instructions, until just tender. Drain the pasta, reserving 50 ml (2 fl oz) of the cooking liquid.

2 Meanwhile, heat a wok or large frying pan, add the pine nuts and toast them over a medium heat, stirring all the time, for 1–2 minutes until lightly brown. Remove the pine nuts and leave to cool.

3 Heat the oil in the frying pan and stir-fry the garlic and chillies for about 30 seconds, or until starting to brown. Add the prawns and stir-fry for 1 minute just to heat them through (any longer and they may become tough).

4 Stir in the pasta, reserved cooking liquid, pine nuts, lemon juice and basil. Season to taste with salt and pepper and heat through before serving.

serves **4**
preparation time **10 minutes**
cooking time **15 minutes**

Seafood pasta

375 g (12 oz) fusilli
25 g (1 oz) butter
125 g (4 oz) cooked peeled
prawns
125 g (4 oz) fresh mussels,
cooked and shelled
125 g (4 oz) squid rings
300 ml (½ pint) single cream
2 tablespoons chopped dill
50 g (2 oz) sweetcorn kernels,
thawed if frozen
25 g (1 oz) oyster
mushrooms, sliced
salt and pepper

1 Cook the pasta in a large saucepan of salted boiling water for 8–12 minutes, or according to packet instructions, until just tender.

2 Meanwhile, melt the butter in a saucepan. Add the cooked prawns and mussels, and the squid rings. Fry for about 3 minutes, stirring from time to time.

3 Stir in the cream, half the chopped dill, the sweetcorn and mushrooms, and heat through. Season with salt and pepper to taste.

4 Drain the pasta and return to the clean pan. Add the seafood sauce and stir carefully. Serve at once, garnished with the remaining chopped dill.

PASTA TIP
You can use ready-prepared, cleaned squid for this recipe or buy whole fresh squid and prepare them yourself. If preparing them yourself, you will need 250 g (8 oz).

serves **4**
preparation time **10 minutes**
cooking time **15 minutes**

Capelli d'angelo
with prawns and brandy

375 g (12 oz) capelli d'angelo
25 g (1 oz) butter
4 plum tomatoes, chopped
2 tablespoons brandy
200 g (7 oz) cooked peeled
    prawns
3 tablespoons double cream
1 tablespoon chopped
    tarragon
salt and pepper

1 Cook the pasta in a large saucepan of salted boiling water for 8–12 minutes, or according to packet instructions, until just tender.

2 Meanwhile, heat the butter in a frying pan over a medium heat and fry the tomatoes for 2–3 minutes until they have softened. Pour in the brandy, turn the heat up to high and cook for 2 minutes.

3 Add the prawns, cream and tarragon and heat through. Season well with salt and pepper. Drain the pasta well. Toss the sauce with the hot pasta and serve immediately.

PASTA TIP
Small prawns are often sweeter than the big tiger prawns, and that's exactly what you want in this dish. Frozen ones are fine, just defrost them before cooking. Make sure you boil off the brandy properly to remove its slightly 'raw' taste before adding the prawns and herbs.

serves **4**
preparation time **15 minutes**
cooking time **12 minutes**

Pasta with prawns
and black beans

375 g (12 oz) tagliatelle
3 tablespoons fermented
　black beans, rinsed
½ teaspoon caster sugar
1 teaspoon sesame oil
6 tablespoons groundnut oil
1 fresh chilli, deseeded and
　finely chopped
2.5 cm (1 inch) piece of fresh
　root ginger, peeled and very
　finely chopped
4 garlic cloves, chopped
500 g (1 lb) peeled prawns
3 tablespoons chopped
　coriander leaves
2 tablespoons rice or wine
　vinegar
salt

1　Cook the pasta in a large saucepan of salted boiling water for 8–12 minutes, or according to packet instructions, until just tender.

2　Meanwhile, mash the beans to a paste with the sugar and sesame oil. Heat 4 tablespoons of the groundnut oil in a wok, until almost smoking. Add the chilli, ginger and garlic and stir-fry for 4–5 seconds.

3　Add the prawns and coriander, and stir-fry for 3 minutes. Add the bean paste, then the rice vinegar. Stir well, then remove from the pan and keep warm.

4　Wipe out the wok and heat the remaining groundnut oil. Drain the pasta, add it to the wok and stir over a medium heat to coat.

5　Transfer the pasta to a serving dish, top with the prawns and serve immediately.

serves **4–6**
preparation time **15 minutes**
cooking time **8–12 minutes**

Fusilli with smoked trout,
asparagus and lemon

250 g (8 oz) **fusilli**
375 g (12 oz) **asparagus
spears, trimmed and cut
into 5 cm (2 inch) lengths**
125 g (4 oz) **frozen peas,
thawed**
2 large **tomatoes, skinned,
deseeded and chopped**
**juice and rind (removed with
a zester in thin narrow
strips) of 1 small lemon**
small handful of **basil leaves,
chopped**
small handful of **parsley
leaves, chopped**
125 ml (4 fl oz) **French
dressing**
250 g (8 oz) **smoked trout
fillets**
salt and pepper

1 Cook the pasta in a large saucepan of salted boiling water for 8–12 minutes, or according to packet instructions, until just tender.

2 Meanwhile, cook the asparagus in a shallow saucepan of boiling water for 4–5 minutes, until almost tender. Drain it in a colander, then cool under cold running water. Drain again thoroughly.

3 Drain the pasta in a colander and rinse under cold running water. Drain thoroughly and transfer to a serving bowl.

4 Add the asparagus, peas, tomatoes, lemon rind, basil and parsley to the pasta. Season well with salt and pepper.

5 Just before serving, add the lemon juice to the salad with the French dressing.

6 Flake the smoked trout into the salad and toss lightly to combine all the ingredients.

PASTA TIP
Smoked trout fillet is widely available in many larger supermarkets and has a delicious flavour that works well with this dish.

serves **4**
preparation time **15 minutes**
cooking time **18–12 minutes**

Prawn linguine
with lemon and chilli

375 g (12 oz) linguine
1 tablespoon olive oil
1 tablespoon butter
1 garlic clove, finely chopped
2 spring onions, thinly sliced
**2 red chillies, seeded and
    thinly sliced**
**425 g (14 oz) raw king prawns,
    shelled with tails left intact**
2 tablespoons lemon juice
**2 tablespoons finely chopped
    coriander leaves**
salt and pepper
coriander leaves, to garnish

1 Cook the pasta in a large pan of salted boiling water for 8–12 minutes, or according to packet instructions, until just tender.

2 Meanwhile, heat the oil and butter in a large frying pan. Add the garlic, spring onions and chillies and stir-fry for 2–3 minutes. Add the prawns and cook briskly for 3–4 minutes, or until they turn pink and are just cooked through.

3 Stir in the lemon juice and coriander leaves, then remove from the heat.

4 Drain the pasta, add it to the prawn mixture, season well and toss together. Serve hot, garnished with coriander leaves.

serves **4**
preparation time **10 minutes**
cooking time **15 minutes**

Squid ink pasta
with monkfish, chilli and spinach

375 g (12 oz) black squid ink
  pasta
200 g (7 oz) monkfish fillet,
  cut into 2.5 cm (1 inch)
  cubes
2 large red chillies, deseeded
  and finely chopped
2 garlic cloves, chopped
2 tablespoons Thai fish sauce
25 g (1 oz) butter
150 g (5 oz) baby spinach
juice of 2 limes
salt
lime wedges, to serve

1 Cook the pasta in a large saucepan of salted boiling water for 8–12 minutes, or according to packet instructions, until just tender.

2 Meanwhile, place the monkfish cubes on a large piece of foil and top with the chillies, garlic and fish sauce. Fold up the edges of the foil and turn them over to seal the parcel. Place on a baking sheet and cook in a preheated oven, 200°C (400°F), Gas Mark 6, for 8–10 minutes until cooked through.

3 Drain the pasta well, add the butter and toss to coat, then toss the contents of the parcel with the hot pasta. Add the spinach and stir until it wilts. Add lime juice and salt to taste and serve immediately with lime wedges.

PASTA TIP
Black squid ink pasta has
a very subtle taste of fish
and looks stunning,
making it the perfect
choice when entertaining
friends or family.

serves **4**
preparation time **13 minutes**
cooking time **17 minutes**

Mussel
and lemon pasta

**1 kg (2 lb) mussels, scrubbed
   and debearded
375 g (12 oz) spaghetti
6 tablespoons olive oil
2 garlic cloves, sliced
1 large red chilli, deseeded
   and chopped
grated rind and juice of
   1 lemon
2 tablespoons water
4 tablespoons chopped
   coriander leaves
salt and pepper**

1 Discard any mussels that are broken or do not shut immediately when sharply tapped with the back of a knife.

2 Cook the pasta in a large pan of salted boiling water for 8–12 minutes, or according to packet instructions, until just tender.

3 Meanwhile, heat the oil in a wok or large frying pan and fry the garlic, chilli and lemon rind, stirring occasionally, for 3 minutes until golden. Remove from the heat.

4 Put the mussels into a large saucepan with the measured water, cover tightly and cook, shaking the pan frequently, for 4 minutes, until the shells have opened. Discard any mussels that remain closed.

5 Drain the pasta. Return the garlic mixture to the heat and stir in the pasta, the mussels and their cooking liquid, the lemon juice and the coriander leaves. Season to taste with salt and pepper, heat through and serve.

serves **4**
preparation time **10 minutes**
cooking time **15 minutes**

Layered tuna lasagne
with rocket

8 no pre-cook lasagne sheets
1 teaspoon olive oil
1 bunch spring onions, sliced
2 courgettes, diced
500 g (1 lb) cherry tomatoes,
    quartered
50 g (2 oz) rocket
2 x 200 g (7 oz) cans tuna in
    water, drained
4 teaspoons ready-made
    pesto
pepper

1 Cook the lasagne sheets in a large saucepan of salted boiling water for 8–12 minutes, or according to packet instructions, until just tender.

2 Meanwhile, heat the oil in a medium frying pan, add the spring onions and courgettes and fry for 3 minutes. Remove from the heat, add the tomatoes and rocket, flake in the tuna and gently toss together.

3 Remove the lasagne sheets with a slotted spoon and drain on kitchen paper.

4 Place a little of the tuna mixture on 4 serving plates and top with a sheet of the cooked lasagne. Spoon the remaining tuna mix over the lasagne, then top with the remaining sheets of lasagne. Top with a teaspoon of pesto and season with plenty of pepper before serving.

PASTA TIP
Try using green lasagne
sheets, which have been
flavoured with spinach,
to add extra variety to
this dish.

serves **4**
preparation time **15 minutes, plus marinating**
cooking time **10 minutes**

Stir-fried monkfish
with noodles

1 egg white, lightly beaten
1 tablespoon dry sherry
1 tablespoon cornflour
750 g (1½ lb) monkfish fillet,
   washed, dried and cubed
125 g (4 oz) egg noodles
2 tablespoons sunflower oil
2 teaspoons sesame oil
1 garlic clove, sliced
2.5 cm (1 inch) piece of fresh
   root ginger, peeled and
   sliced
2 teaspoons grated orange
   rind
1 small leek, sliced
1 red pepper, cored, deseeded
   and sliced
50 g (2 oz) canned water
   chestnuts, drained and
   sliced
50 g (2 oz) bean sprouts
chopped coriander leaves,
   to garnish

sauce
6 tablespoons vegetable or
   chicken stock
6 tablespoons fresh orange
   juice
2 tablespoons dark soy sauce
1 tablespoon rice or wine
   vinegar
2 teaspoons clear honey
pepper

1 Blend the egg white, sherry and cornflour together in a dish, add the monkfish and toss well. Set aside for several hours or overnight.

2 Remove the monkfish from its marinade using a slotted spoon. Combine all the sauce ingredients and set aside. Cook the noodles in a saucepan of salted boiling water for 4 minutes, or according to packet instructions, separating them with a fork as they cook, then drain well.

3 Heat the sunflower and sesame oils in a wok or large frying pan and stir-fry the monkfish over a high heat for 2 minutes, until golden. Remove from the pan with the cleaned slotted spoon.

4 Add the garlic, ginger, orange rind, leek and red pepper to the wok and stir-fry for 3 minutes. Add the water chestnuts, bean sprouts, noodles, sauce and monkfish. Simmer gently for 2 minutes, until the monkfish and all the vegetables are heated through. Garnish with coriander leaves and serve.

serves **4**
preparation time **15 minutes**
cooking time **8–12 minutes**

Spicy tuna steak
with tagliatelle

375 g (12 oz) green tagliatelle
25 g (1 oz) almonds
2 large green chillies,
deseeded and roughly
chopped
25 g (1 oz) fresh coriander
with roots
1 large garlic clove, roughly
chopped
2 tablespoons lime juice
5 tablespoons olive oil
4 tuna steaks, about 150 g
(5 oz) each
salt
lime wedges, to serve

1 Cook the pasta in a large saucepan of salted boiling water for 8–12 minutes, or according to packet instructions, until just tender.

2 Meanwhile, spread the almonds on a baking sheet and place under a hot grill for a few minutes until lightly toasted.

3 Place the chillies, coriander, garlic, almonds and lime juice in a food processor or blender and blend for 10 seconds. Blend again while drizzling in the oil. Season with salt.

4 Cook the tuna in a preheated ridged grill pan or frying pan for 30 seconds on each side so it is still pink in the centre. Slice the tuna steaks in half.

5 Drain the pasta and toss it with two-thirds of the coriander sauce and divide it between four plates. Top each portion with two pieces of tuna, a dollop of the remaining sauce and some lime wedges.

PASTA TIP
You need a very hot pan to sear tuna, and the cooking time depends on the thickness of the steak. Tuna should be served still pink in the middle, so it is better to cook the fish for a shorter time, then return it to the pan if it is not cooked to your liking. Overcooking will ruin its lovely taste and texture.

Vegetarian

Pasta has a natural affinity with vegetables, cheese, eggs and cream – making it the perfect base for vegetarian meals. But with choices such as Fusilli with Goats' Cheese and Watercress Pesto and Spaghetti with Charred Asparagus, Lemon and Basil you might find meat eaters wanting some too!

serves **4**
preparation time **5 minutes**
cooking time **8–12 minutes**

Fusilli with goats'
cheese and watercress pesto

375 g (12 oz) **fusilli**
50 g (2 oz) **pine nuts, plus**
extra to garnish
1 **garlic clove, roughly**
chopped
150 g (5 oz) **watercress**
7 **tablespoons extra virgin**
olive oil
150 g (5 oz) **crumbly goats'**
cheese, plus extra to
garnish
salt and pepper

1 Cook the pasta in a large saucepan of salted boiling water for 8–12 minutes, or according to packet instructions, until just tender.

2 Meanwhile, heat a nonstick frying pan, add the pine nuts and toast them over a medium heat, stirring all the time, for 1–2 minutes until lightly brown.

3 Place the pine nuts, garlic and watercress in a food processor or blender with a generous pinch of salt. Blend for 15 seconds until roughly chopped, then blend for another 20 seconds as you drizzle in the olive oil. Crumble in the goats' cheese and stir thoroughly. Season with pepper.

4 Drain the pasta well then stir the pesto into the hot pasta. Divide it between 4 plates to serve and scatter with extra goats' cheese and pine nuts.

PASTA TIP
Look out for organic watercress for this twist on the classic basil pesto, which uses watercress and goats' cheese in place of the classic basil and Parmesan. Be careful not to overblend the watercress and pine nuts because the pesto is best when it still retains some texture.

serves **4**
preparation time **10 minutes**
cooking time **17–25 minutes**

Summer vegetable fettuccine

250 g (8 oz) asparagus,
  trimmed and cut into
  5 cm (2 inch) lengths
125 g (4 oz) sugar snap peas
400 g (13 oz) fettuccine
1 tablespoon olive oil
1 small onion, finely chopped
1 garlic clove, finely chopped
200 g (7 oz) baby courgettes,
  halved lengthways
150 g (5 oz) button
  mushrooms, halved
4 tablespoons lemon juice
2 teaspoons chopped
  tarragon
2 teaspoons chopped parsley
100 g (3½ oz) smoked
  mozzarella cheese, diced
salt and pepper
garlic bread, to serve

1 Bring a saucepan of water to the boil. Add the asparagus and sugar snap peas and boil for 3–4 minutes, then drain and refresh with cold water. Drain well and set aside.

2 Cook the pasta in a large saucepan of salted boiling water for 8–12 minutes, or according to packet instructions, until just tender.

3 Meanwhile, heat the oil in a large frying pan. Add the onion and garlic, and cook gently for 2–3 minutes. Add the courgettes and mushrooms and stir-fry for 3–4 minutes. Stir in the asparagus and sugar snap peas and cook for 1–2 minutes before adding the lemon juice, tarragon and parsley.

4 Drain the pasta and return it to the pan. Add the vegetable mixture and mozzarella and season to taste. Toss lightly to mix, then serve at once with hot garlic bread.

serves **4–6**
preparation time **12 minutes**
cooking time **8–12 minutes**

Pesto Trapanese

500–750 g (1–1½ lb) fusilli
3 ripe tomatoes
4 garlic cloves
50 g (2 oz) basil leaves, plus
    extra to garnish
125 g (4 oz) blanched
    almonds, toasted
150 ml (¼ pint) olive oil
salt and pepper

1 Cook the pasta in a large saucepan of salted boiling water for 8–12 minutes, or according to packet instructions, until just tender.

2 Meanwhile, place all the remaining ingredients in a food processor or blender and blend until smooth. Alternatively, finely chop the tomatoes, garlic, basil and almonds by hand, and stir in the olive oil to give a chunkier sauce. Season to taste with salt and pepper.

3 Drain the pasta well, then toss the pesto with it. The pesto will be warmed by the heat of the pasta. Garnish with a few basil leaves.

PASTA TIP
The pesto can be prepared in advance, if liked. Once prepared, spoon the pesto into a jar, pour a layer of olive oil over the surface and chill until required. To use this sauce, let it come to room temperature then stir it into freshly cooked pasta.

serves **4**
preparation time **10 minutes**
cooking time **8–10 minutes**

Chilli and coriander linguine
with cashew nut pesto

400 g (13 oz) linguine
50 g (2 oz) coriander leaves,
coarsely chopped
2 garlic cloves, coarsely
chopped
50 g (2 oz) roasted cashew
nuts
1 green chilli, deseeded
and coarsely chopped
125 ml (4 fl oz) olive oil
50 g (2 oz) freshly grated
Parmesan cheese
salt and pepper

to serve
crusty bread
crisp green salad

1 Cook the pasta in a large saucepan of salted boiling water for 8–12 minutes, or according to packet instructions, until just tender.

2 Meanwhile, process the coriander, garlic, cashew nuts, chilli and olive oil in a food processor or blender until fairly smooth and creamy. Add the cheese and process for a few seconds. Transfer the pesto to a bowl, season well and set aside.

3 Drain the pasta and return it to the pan. Add the pesto and mix well. Serve at once with crusty bread and a crisp salad.

serves **4**
preparation time **15–20 minutes**
cooking time **5–12 minutes**

Tagliatelle al pesto

500 g (1 lb) tagliatelle
salt and pepper
50 g (2 oz) freshly grated
  Parmesan cheese, to serve

pesto
50 g (2 oz) pine nuts
1 garlic clove, crushed
50 g (2 oz) basil leaves
75 g (3 oz) freshly grated
  Parmesan cheese
juice of ½ lemon
125 ml (4 fl oz) olive oil

1 Cook the pasta in a large saucepan of salted boiling water for 8–12 minutes, or according to packet instructions, until just tender.

2 Meanwhile, make the pesto. Spread the pine nuts on a baking sheet and place in a preheated oven, 220°C (425°F), Gas Mark 7, for 3–5 minutes, until golden. Keep checking them to make sure that they do not burn.

3 Pound the pine nuts with the garlic to a thick paste using a pestle and mortar. Alternatively, use a food processor or blender. Tear the basil leaves into shreds and add to the pine nut mixture. Continue pounding or processing until you have a thick green paste.

4 Drain the pasta and keep it warm. Transfer the pesto to a bowl (if using a mortar) and stir in the freshly grated Parmesan and lemon juice. Add the olive oil, a little at a time, beating well in between each addition.

5 Sprinkle with pepper and toss the pasta lightly with the pesto. Serve sprinkled with freshly grated Parmesan.

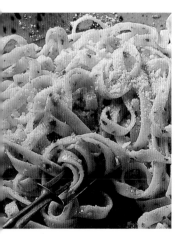

serves **4**
preparation time **15 minutes**
cooking time **8–12 minutes**

Penne, broad bean
and feta cheese salad

400 g (13 oz) penne
400 g (13 oz) fresh or frozen
broad beans
100 g (3½ oz) sun-dried
tomatoes in oil, drained
and roughly chopped
handful of mixed herbs, such
as parsley, tarragon, chervil
and chives, roughly
chopped
100 g (3½ oz) feta cheese,
crumbled or roughly
chopped
salt and pepper

dressing
4 tablespoons extra virgin
olive oil
2 tablespoons sherry vinegar
1 teaspoon wholegrain
mustard

1 Cook the pasta in a large saucepan of salted boiling water for 8–12 minutes, or according to packet instructions, until just tender.

2 Meanwhile, cook the broad beans in a separate saucepan of lightly salted boiling water for 4–5 minutes, or until just tender. Drain and plunge into ice-cold water to cool. Peel away and discard the outer shells.

3 Whisk the dressing ingredients together in a small bowl and season to taste with salt and pepper.

4 Drain the pasta, rinse with cold water and drain again. Place the beans in a serving dish and stir in the pasta, tomatoes and herbs. Toss with the dressing. Season with freshly ground black pepper and sprinkle over the feta.

serves **4**
preparation time **10 minutes**
cooking time **12 minutes**

Pasta with broad beans
and artichoke pesto

375 g (12 oz) penne
375 g (12 oz) fresh or frozen
  broad beans

pesto
75 g (3 oz) marinated charred
  artichokes, roughly
  chopped
1 garlic clove, chopped
15 g (½ oz) parsley, chopped
1 tablespoon pine nuts
15 g (½ oz) pecorino cheese,
  grated, plus extra to serve
150 ml (¼ pint) extra virgin
  olive oil
salt and pepper

1 Cook the pasta in a large saucepan of salted boiling water for 8–12 minutes, or according to packet instructions, until just tender.

2 Meanwhile, blanch the broad beans in a pan of lightly salted boiling water for 3 minutes. Drain and set aside.

3 Put the artichokes, garlic, parsley and pine nuts in a food processor or blender and process until fairly smooth. Transfer the mixture to a bowl and stir in the pecorino and oil and season to taste with salt and pepper.

4 Drain the pasta, reserving 4 tablespoons of the cooking liquid, and return it to the pan. Add the pesto, broad beans and reserved cooking liquid and season to taste with pepper. Toss over a medium heat until warmed through. Serve with extra grated pecorino.

PASTA TIP
Marinated charred artichokes are often sold in jars. If you can't find them, use canned artichoke hearts instead.

serves **4**
preparation time **10 minutes**
cooking time **20 minutes**

Spaghetti with charred asparagus,
lemon and basil

375 g (12 oz) spaghetti
500 g (1 lb) thin asparagus
  spears or broccoli florets
3–4 tablespoons extra virgin
  olive oil
4 tablespoons lemon juice
2 garlic cloves, roughly
  chopped
¼–½ teaspoon dried crushed
  chillies
40 g (1½ oz) basil leaves
25 g (1 oz) freshly grated
  Parmesan cheese, plus
  extra to serve
salt and pepper

1 Cook the pasta in a large saucepan of salted boiling water for 8–12 minutes, or according to packet instructions, until just tender.

2 Meanwhile, brush the asparagus spears with a little oil and cook under a preheated hot grill for 3–6 minutes until charred and tender. Toss with a little more oil and half the lemon juice, season to taste with salt and pepper, and keep warm.

3 Just before the pasta is cooked, heat the remaining oil in a large frying pan and sauté the garlic with a little salt for 3–4 minutes, or until softened but not browned. Add the chillies and asparagus and heat through.

4 Drain the pasta, reserving 4 tablespoons of the cooking liquid, and return it to the pan. Add the asparagus, basil, the remaining lemon juice, the cooking liquid and freshly grated Parmesan. Season to taste with pepper and serve with extra Parmesan.

serves **4**
preparation time **5 minutes**
cooking time **17 minutes**

Pasta with radicchio
and cheese crumbs

375 g (12 oz) spaghetti
150 g (5 oz) butter
50 g (2 oz) fresh white
   breadcrumbs
25 g (1 oz) freshly grated
   Parmesan cheese
2 shallots, finely chopped
1 garlic clove, sliced
1 head radicchio, shredded
dash of lemon juice
salt and pepper

1 Cook the pasta in a large saucepan of salted boiling water for 8–12 minutes, or according to packet instructions, until just tender.

2 Meanwhile, melt half the butter in a frying pan and fry the breadcrumbs, stirring frequently, for about 5 minutes, until evenly golden and crisp. Transfer the crumbs to a bowl, cool slightly and add the Parmesan.

3 Heat the remaining butter in a wok or large frying pan and fry the shallots and garlic, stirring occasionally, for 5 minutes, until softened. Add the radicchio to the pan with a little lemon juice and season to taste with salt and pepper. Stir over a low heat for about 2 minutes, until the radicchio has wilted.

4 Drain the pasta, reserving 2 tablespoons of the cooking liquid. Add the pasta and liquid to the radicchio mixture, toss until heated through and serve topped with the cheese crumbs.

serves **4**
preparation time **8 minutes**
cooking time **8–12 minutes**

Rigatoni with courgettes,
feta and lemon thyme

375 g (12 oz) rigatoni
3 courgettes, cut into 1 cm
   (½ inch) slices
6 tablespoons olive oil
2 tablespoons lemon juice
2 lemon thyme sprigs
200 g (7 oz) feta cheese, cubed
12 pitted green olives, roughly
   chopped
salt and pepper
Parmesan cheese shavings,
   to serve

1 Cook the pasta in a large saucepan of salted boiling water for 8–12 minutes, or according to packet instructions, until just tender.

2 Meanwhile, place the courgettes in a large bowl and toss with 1 tablespoon of the oil. Cook the courgette slices on a preheated ridged grill pan for 2–3 minutes on each side until tender.

3 Return the courgette slices to the bowl, drizzle with the remaining olive oil and the lemon juice, and scatter over the lemon thyme. Season with salt and pepper.

4 Drain the pasta and add it to the bowl along with the feta and olives. Toss well to combine then serve with Parmesan shavings.

PASTA TIP
Lemon thyme has a heady, floral aroma and flavour that are just wonderful in this dish. If you can't find it, use regular thyme instead and add some grated lemon rind.

serves **6**
preparation time **15 minutes**
cooking time **8–12 minutes**

Carter's pasta

750 g (1½ lb) spaghetti
6 ripe tomatoes, about 750 g
   (1½ lb)
4–5 garlic cloves
50 g (2 oz) basil leaves
pinch of dried crushed chillies
150 ml (¼ pint) olive oil
125 g (4 oz) salted ricotta or
   pecorino cheese, grated,
   plus extra to serve
salt

1 Cook the pasta in a large saucepan of salted boiling water for 8–12 minutes, or according to packet instructions, until just tender.

2 Meanwhile, skin and chop the tomatoes, retaining all the juice, and transfer them to a bowl.

3 Put the garlic, basil, chillies and a pinch of salt into a food processor or blender and process until smooth, then add the oil slowly until the sauce becomes smooth again. Alternatively, use a pestle and mortar. Mix the purée into the chopped tomatoes.

4 Drain the pasta, reserving a couple of spoonfuls of the cooking water. Tip the spaghetti into a serving bowl, toss with half of the cheese and the cooking liquid, then mix in the sauce. Sprinkle with the remaining cheese. Serve with a small bowl of grated cheese handed around separately.

PASTA TIP
This pasta dish was a staple food of Sicilian cart drivers, quickly rustled up by the side of the road with a few basic ingredients – tomatoes, garlic, olive oil, spaghetti and salted ricotta, which kept well because it was preserved. The recipe has been refined somewhat to suit modern, indoor kitchens.

serves **4**
preparation time **10 minutes**
cooking time **4 minutes**

Tomato tagliatelle with mushrooms
and pecan nuts

**250 g (8 oz) fresh tomato
tagliatelle**
25 g (1 oz) butter
**250 g (8 oz) mixed
mushrooms, sliced if large**
25 g (1 oz) pecan nuts, halved
salt and pepper

1 Cook the pasta in a large saucepan of salted boiling water for 4 minutes, or according to packet instructions, until just tender.

2 Meanwhile, melt the butter in a frying pan and fry the mushrooms and pecan nuts for 2 minutes, stirring constantly. Add salt and pepper to taste.

3 Drain the pasta and transfer it to a warmed serving bowl. Add the mushroom and pecan nut mixture and toss well to mix with the pasta. Season to taste with salt and pepper.

serves **4**
preparation time **10 minutes**
cooking time **12 minutes**

Field mushroom tortellini

300 g (10 oz) **tortellini**
25 g (1 oz) **butter**
500 g (1 lb) **field mushrooms,
    thinly sliced**
3 **shallots, finely chopped**
2 tablespoons **chopped
    oregano**
250 ml (8 fl oz) **double cream**
salt and pepper
25 g (1 oz) **freshly grated
    Parmesan cheese, to serve**

1 Cook the pasta in a large saucepan of salted boiling water for 8–12 minutes, or according to packet instructions, until just tender.

2 Meanwhile, melt the butter in a large frying pan and fry the mushrooms and shallots for 5 minutes.

3 Reduce the heat and stir in two-thirds of the oregano, the cream and salt and pepper to taste. Simmer gently for about 5 minutes, or until the cream has started to thicken.

4 Drain the pasta and return it to the saucepan. Stir in the cream sauce and serve with freshly grated Parmesan. Garnish with the remaining oregano.

PASTA TIP
Large field mushrooms seem to have a more 'mushroomy' taste than their cultivated cousins. They are quite widely available, but if you don't have any on hand, you could substitute ordinary button mushrooms, and add a few dried porcini, soaked in a little boiling water, to add extra zing to the taste.

serves **4**
preparation time **20 minutes, plus standing**
cooking time **18–22 minutes**

Mushroom and mozzarella lasagne stacks

8 no pre-cook lasagne sheets
2 tablespoons olive oil
50 g (2 oz) butter
2 onions, chopped
2 garlic cloves, chopped
500 g (1 lb) mushrooms,
trimmed and sliced
4 tablespoons double cream
4 tablespoons dry white wine
1 teaspoon chopped thyme
2 red peppers, skinned (see
page 41), cored, deseeded
and thickly sliced
125 g (4 oz) baby spinach
125 g (4 oz) mozzarella cheese
salt and pepper
50 g (2 oz) Parmesan cheese
shavings

1 Cook the lasagne sheets in a large saucepan of salted boiling water for 8–12 minutes, or according to packet instructions, until just tender.

2 Meanwhile, heat the oil and butter in a saucepan, add the onions and sauté for 3 minutes. Add the garlic and cook for 1 minute. Add the mushrooms, turn up the heat and cook for 5 minutes.

3 Drain the lasagne and keep warm. Add the cream, wine and thyme to the mushroom mixture, season with salt and pepper and simmer for 4 minutes.

4 Place 4 sheets of lasagne in a well-oiled 1.8 litre (3 pint) ovenproof dish. Place a generous spoonful of mushroom mixture on each piece of lasagne, add some red pepper slices and half of the spinach, and place another piece of lasagne on top. Then add the remaining spinach, a little more mushroom mixture and top with a slice of mozzarella. Finish with the Parmesan shavings. Place the dish under a preheated hot grill and cook for 5 minutes until the Parmesan is bubbling.

serves **4**
preparation time **30 minutes, plus resting the dough**
cooking time **10 minutes**

Spinach and ricotta ravioli

pasta
200 g (7 oz) Farina Bianco 00 or
Tipo 00 flour
pinch of salt
1 tablespoon olive oil
2 large eggs, beaten

filling
750 g (1½ lb) fresh spinach
175 g (6 oz) fresh ricotta or
curd cheese
½ teaspoon grated nutmeg
1 teaspoon salt
pepper
1 egg, beaten

to serve
50 g (2 oz) butter, diced
25 g (1 oz) freshly grated
Parmesan cheese

1 Sift the flour and salt on to a work surface and make a well in the centre. Pour in the oil and beaten eggs and gradually mix into the flour. Once combined, bring the dough together and shape into a ball. Knead on a floured work surface for about 10 minutes until smooth and elastic. Wrap in clingfilm and leave to rest at room temperature for 30 minutes.

2 Place the spinach in a large saucepan with a little water. Cook, covered, over a medium heat, shaking the pan occasionally, for 3–4 minutes until the spinach is just wilted. Drain in a colander, pressing out all the moisture. Put the spinach and ricotta in a food processor with the nutmeg, salt and pepper to taste and process until smooth. Cover and chill.

3 Unwrap the dough and cut it in half. Roll each half on a very lightly floured surface as thinly as possible to make two 30 cm (12 inch) squares. Spoon small mounds of the filling in even rows on one sheet of pasta, spacing them at 4 cm (1½ inch) intervals. Brush the spaces of dough between the mounds with beaten egg. Using a rolling pin, lift the remaining sheet of pasta over the sheet with the filling. Press down firmly between the mounds of filling. Cut the pasta into squares with a serrated pastry cutter or a sharp knife.

4 Bring a large saucepan of salted water to the boil, add a dash of olive oil and carefully add the ravioli. Bring back to the boil, turn off the heat and cover. Leave for 5 minutes, then drain the ravioli well and return them to the pan, add the butter and toss to melt. Serve with freshly grated Parmesan.

serves **4**
preparation time **35 minutes, plus resting the dough**
cooking time **13 minutes**

Herb and wild mushroom ravioli

pasta
200 g (7 oz) Farina Bianco 00
   or Tipo 00 flour
pinch of salt
1 tablespoon olive oil
2 large eggs, beaten
4 tablespoons chopped
   mixed tarragon, marjoram
   and parsley

filling
50 g (2 oz) butter
2 shallots, finely chopped
250 g (8 oz) mixed wild
   mushrooms, chopped
   finely
25 g (1 oz) Greek-style black
   olives, pitted and finely
   chopped
4 sun-dried tomato halves in
   oil, drained and finely
   chopped
1 tablespoon dry Marsala
freshly grated nutmeg
salt and pepper
1 egg, beaten

to serve
50 g (2 oz) butter, diced
Parmesan cheese shavings

1 Sift the flour and salt in a mound on a work surface and make a well in the centre. Pour in the oil and beaten eggs, then sprinkle over the herbs, and gradually mix into the flour. Once combined, bring the dough together and shape into a ball. Knead on a floured work surface for about 10 minutes until smooth and elastic. Wrap in clingfilm and leave to rest at room temperature for 30 minutes.

2 Melt the butter in a frying pan, add the shallots and cook for 5 minutes. Stir in the mushrooms, olives and sun-dried tomatoes and cook, stirring, over a high heat for about 2 minutes. Sprinkle with the dry Marsala and cook for 1 minute longer. Season with salt, pepper and grated nutmeg.

3 Unwrap the dough and cut it in half. Roll each half on a very lightly floured surface as thinly as possible to make two 30 cm (12 inch) squares. Place 16 heaped spoonfuls of filling on one sheet of pasta in 4 even rows, spacing them at 4 cm (1½ inch) intervals. Brush the spaces of dough between the mounds with beaten egg. With a rolling pin, lift the remaining sheet of pasta over the dough with the filling. Press down firmly between the mounds of filling. Cut the pasta into squares with a serrated pastry cutter or a sharp knife.

4 Bring a large saucepan of salted water to the boil, add a dash of olive oil and carefully add the ravioli. Bring back to the boil, turn off the heat and cover the pan. Leave for 5 minutes, then drain the ravioli well and return them to the pan, add the butter and toss to melt. Serve with Parmesan shavings.

serves **4**
preparation time **45 minutes, plus resting the dough**
cooking time **5 minutes**

Ricotta ravioli
with olives and truffles

pasta
**200 g (7 oz) Farina Bianco 00
or Tipo 00 flour**
pinch of salt
1 tablespoon olive oil
2 large eggs, beaten

filling
200 g (7 oz) ricotta cheese
2 egg yolks, lightly beaten
**75 g (3 oz) fontina cheese,
finely grated**
**50 g (2 oz) black truffles,
finely chopped**
**50 g (2 oz) pitted black olives,
finely chopped**
2 tablespoons chopped basil
1 tablespoon truffle oil
pinch of ground nutmeg
salt and pepper

to serve
truffle shavings
truffle oil
rocket leaves
pepper

1 Sift the flour and salt on to a work surface and make a well in the centre. Pour in the oil and beaten eggs and gradually mix into the flour. Once combined, bring the dough together and shape into a ball. Knead on a floured work surface for about 10 minutes until smooth and elastic. Wrap in clingfilm and leave to rest at room temperature for 30 minutes.

2 Unwrap the dough and cut it in half. Roll each half on a very lightly floured surface as thinly as possible to make two 30 cm (12 inch) squares.

3 Mix together all the filling ingredients and season with salt and pepper. Place small teaspoons of the filling on one of the pasta sheets, about 5 cm (2 inches) apart, moisten the edges of the dough and put the second sheet on top. Push down along the moistened edges so that each mound of filling is sealed well. Use a serrated pastry cutter to cut the pasta into 5 cm (2 inch) squares.

4 Bring a large saucepan of salted water to the boil, add a dash of olive oil and carefully add the ravioli. Bring back to the boil, turn off the heat and cover. Leave for 5 minutes, then drain and serve with truffle shavings, a drizzle of truffle oil, some rocket leaves and a dusting of fresh, coarsely ground black pepper.

serves **4**
preparation time **2 minutes**
cooking time **8–12 minutes**

Ravioli
with burnt sage butter

**500 g (1 lb) good-quality fresh
or home-made ravioli**
50 g (2 oz) butter
50 g (2 oz) pine nuts
15 sage leaves, sliced
2 tablespoons lemon juice
salt
**freshly grated Parmesan
cheese, to serve**

1 Cook the pasta in a large saucepan of salted boiling water for 8–12 minutes, or according to packet instructions, until just tender.

2 Meanwhile, heat the butter in a frying pan over a medium heat and add the pine nuts and sage leaves. Stir until the nuts are light brown and the butter is pale golden. Have the lemon juice to hand and, once the butter starts turning brown, turn off the heat and quickly pour in the lemon juice.

3 Drain the pasta well and divide between 4 warmed plates. Season the butter with salt and pour over the ravioli. Scatter with freshly grated Parmesan and serve immediately.

PASTA TIP
Burnt butter tastes fantastic and is one of the simplest things to make, but the timing is absolutely crucial. You need only to brown the butter a little, so once you see it turning, add the lemon juice to stop it cooking any further.

Index

Acknowledgements

Executive Editor Nicky Hill
Project Editor Emma Pattison
Executive Art Editor Karen Sawyer
Design Cobalt id
Picture Researcher Sophie Delpech
Production Controller Nigel Reed

Octopus Publishing Group Limited/Jean Cazals 48; /Stephen Conroy 1, 17, 20, 23, 27, 31; /Gus Filgate 5, 122; /David Jordan 3, 74; /Graham Kirk 105; /William Lingwood 39, 51, 59, 76, 85, 90, 97, 98–99, 107, 113, 125; /David Loftus 119; /Neil Mersh 101; /James Murphy 40, 78, 83, 116; /Lis Parsons 2, 65, 89; /William Reavell 60–61, 66; /Simon Smith 36; /Ian Wallace 4, 6, 7 background, 8, 11, 12–13, 28, 29, 43, 69, 81, 103, 110, 115, 120; /Philip Webb 10 background, 32, 33, 34–35, 37, 44, 46–47, 53, 54, 72–73, 95.